T0304571

THE RUST OF HISTORY

the selected poems of

SOTERO RIVERA AVILÉS

translated from Spanish by

RAQUEL SALAS RIVERA

THE RUST OF HISTORY

the selected poems of

SOTERO RIVERA AVILÉS

translated from Spanish by

RAQUEL SALAS RIVERA

ISBN 978-1-949918-04-5
First edition.

© Family of Sotero Rivera Avilés.

English translation © 2022 Raquel Salas Rivera.
All rights reserved.

No part of this publication may be reproduced or transmitted in any form
or by any means, electronic or mechanical, including photocopying,
recording, or any information storage or retrieval system, without
permission in writing from the publisher.

Published by:
Circumference Books
85 East End Avenue #14F
New York, New York 10028
www.circumferencebooks.com

Distributed by:
Small Press Distribution (SPD)
1341 Seventh Street
Berkeley, California 94710-1409
www.spdbooks.org

Printed by K⌀PA® *www.kopa.eu*

Contents

Journal of Earth and Man *continued*

nada es olvido mientras existan huellas

Sotero Rivera Avilés

nothing is forgotten as long as there are tracks

Sotero Rivera Avilés

EL PUEBLO OBSCURO Y
UNA PUERTA AL JARDÍN

FECHA DESCONOCIDA

A

FRANCIS SANTIAGO
WILLIAM EVANS
GILBERTO ARROYO

. . . porque estoy triste y viajo,
y conozco la tierra y estoy triste.

Pablo Neruda

THE DARK TOWN AND
A GATE TO THE GARDEN

UNKNOWN DATE

FOR
FRANCIS SANTIAGO
WILLIAM EVANS
GILBERTO ARROYO

…because I am sad and travel,
and know the earth and am sad.

Pablo Neruda

Preámbulo

Cae el libro —
los brazos ya no quieren soportar las palabras.
La luz cae igualmente de mis dedos
y el cuarto se estremece,
                              de pronto, entre sombras.

Y noto el vaho muriente de las últimas lámparas
                                   llegar a mi ventana,
como luz de un entierro
                        lejano por la noche,
como humo de tabaco
de hombres sin tierra alguna cavilando la niebla.

Se derraman entonces los años y las noches —
los días perdidos en el Pueblo Obscuro —,
cuando la lluvia hablaba
de un muchacho sin tiempo en un cuerpo de olvido.

Preamble

The book falls —
the arms are already tired of holding words.
Light also falls from my fingers,
and the room shudders,
                                suddenly, amidst shadows.

I notice the last lamps whose dying vapor
                                reaches my window,
like light from a burial,
                                distant and nocturnal,
like tobacco smoke
from landless men who ponder the mist.

That's when they spill, years and nights —
the days lost in the Dark Town —,
when the rain spoke
of a timeless boy in memory's neglectful body.

Noche del pueblo

Duerme el pueblo — la ilusión gotea;
por las calles más pobres deambulan hombres ebrios;
algún perro rastrea su acostumbrada acera.

("Son las once", me digo,
y escondo las manos en los bolsillos).
Duerme el cura y la iglesia la inválida alcaldía no estira sus campanas;
no ronda el policía, ni aparecen los trenes;
solo un borracho agrio descubro entre las sombras.

Los comerciantes roncan su mezquina riqueza;
muchachas de colegio sueñan con vanas formas;
van y vienen ladridos.
"¿Qué soñarán los pobres?" me pregunto amargado.

Tristeza de existir repetido y cansado,
con gente abandonada y de grises encuentros.
Tristeza de vivir en este pueblo muerto.

The Town's Night

The town sleeps—illusion drips;
down the poorest streets roam wasted men;
some dog tracks his accustomed pavement.

("It's eleven," I tell myself,
and hide my hands in their pockets).
Priest and church are asleep the invalid town hall
    doesn't stretch its bells;
police don't make rounds, trains don't appear;
I discover only a sour drunk amidst shadows.

Merchants snore their meager wealth;
schoolgirls dream of vain forms;
barks come and go.
"What dreams visit the poor?" I bitterly wonder.

The sadness of existing repeated and worn,
among people abandoned and made of gray encounters.
The sadness of living in this dead town.

El pueblo oscuro

Amenazado se levanta el pueblo,
asaltando tiendas y cafetines sucios,
invadiendo el correo y los choferes públicos—
abiertos al comercio pequeño de los pobres.

(Mira el mercado, los verduleros verdes,
mira los rotos carboneros.)

Los muchachos de escuela invaden el aire;
van embistiendo el sol,
con rostros de amapolas y pomarrosas tiernas,
hablando sus amores y nuevas ansiedades.

...Y las mujeres de las fábricas
con sus mejores chismes
y los que hablan de colegios
amordazando vanidades.

Así echó a un lado su obscuridad el pueblo—
con su jauría temprana de sucesos varios
ladrando a los enfermos o a los jíbaros mansos.

Sin embargo, el día rueda
y las calles
se van muriendo como niños pálidos
poco a poco roídos por una fiebre espesa.

(continued)

The Dark Town

The town rises threatened,
raiding stores and dirty cafetines,
invading the post office and public cars—
open to the poor's small exchanges.

(Look at the market, the green greengrocer,
look at the broken charcoal burners.)

Schoolboys invade the air;
start charging against the sun,
with tender hibiscus and rose apple faces,
discussing their loves and latest angsts.

... And the factory women
with their best gossip
and those who speak of schools
muzzling vainness.

This is how the town put its darkness aside—
with its early dog pack of varied events
barking at the sick or jíbaros meek.

Still, the day rolls on
and the roads
start dying like pale children
bit by bit gnawed by a thick fever.

(continued)

Llega la tarde y la noche tiende
sus mosquiteros amarillos,
y todo aquello antes presagiando
un pueblo caminando a lo infinito,
se muere en un difícil
olor a cine alborotado
y cafetines mordidos, con hombres
que solo hablan de livianos ratos
con mujeres abiertas
a todos los hoteles o a la orilla de barcos.

Los más jóvenes repartirán sus besos en el cine
o en bancas descuidadas,
y ni aun los prohibidos
apretaran sus corazones con recato
al encontrarse por corredores o pasillos.

        *   *   *

La plaza con sus mismos paseos,
con su mismo abandono,
con sus mismas parejas y repeticiones.

El desordenado cinematógrafo,
donde acuden los novios a tocarse los cuerpos
y la gente solitaria se ilusiona
con aquello que nunca les sucede.

El mercado, las tiendas de quincalla,
el melancólico hospital con sus pacientes,
pero sin un doctor en la modorra de los montes.

(continued)

Afternoon arrives and night hangs
its yellow mosquito nets,
and all that had previously foretold
a town headed toward infinity,
dies in a difficult
smell of rowdy cinema
and bitten cafetines, with men
that only speak of fun times
with women open
to hotels or the ship-filled shore
or the shores of ships.

The youngest will give out kisses at the movies
or on unattended benches,
and not even those who are banned
will squeeze their hearts modestly
when meeting in corridors or halls.

     *   *   *

The plaza with its same walkways,
with its same abandon,
with its same couples and repetitions.

The disorderly cinematheque
where couples flee to touch bodies
and loners get carried away
with what never happens.

The market, the hardware stores,
the melancholy hospital with its patients,
but doctorless in the drowsiness of mountains.

(continued)

El calor, la terrible pobreza,
el lento paso de los días,
el castigo de cárcel para el hombre
que no es amigo de la policía.

Todo esto me liquida el alma,
me cubre de estropajos,
de materias viscosas, mal olientes,
de fastidios, de sierpes, de cansancio,
de una tristeza triste como tumbas
inscritas con la letra de mi llanto.

  * * *

Que engaño, Pueblo mío,
son tus sitios para ofrecimientos,
donde solo esa gente
que nunca ha entendido ni respetan
la palabra Cultura
suben a las tribunas.

¿Dónde, dónde podrán marcharse
los que lloran bajo la lluvia?
Y entienden que los ricos solo saben
mostrar listas de deudas a los pobres,
o preocuparse por no morir de cáncer.

Y obscuros religiosos
que tratan de escapar de alguien llamado el Diablo
sirviendo misa y amonestando débiles.

(continued)

Heat, terrible poverty,
the slow passage of time,
prison as punishment for the man
who never befriended the police.

All this liquefies my soul,
covers me with scouring pads,
with viscous, fetid matter,
with nuisances, with serpents, with fatigue,
with a sad sadness like tombs,
my grief's handwritten inscription.

*　*　*

What deceit, my Town,
are your places of offering,
where only those
who disrespect or misuse
the word Culture
climb to the podium.

Where, where can they go,
those who cry in the rain?
Those who see that the rich only
know how to list debts for the poor,
or worry about cancer.

And the shrouded religious folk
try to escape some so-and-so called the Devil
offering mass and admonishing the weak.

(continued)

Religiosos vacíos
que no conocen las fuertes súplicas del amor
cuando la llevan los pobres en sus ropas
rasgadas, olorosas a tierra y cansado dolor.
Religiosos vacíos, secos, hasta amargos,
cerrados al verdadero dolor de nuestro pueblo.

Ay, Pueblo Oscuro mío—
guitarra rota sobre mi corazón—
todo lo hemos perdido y nos hemos quedado
con los ojos ausentes
y llenos de cristales rotos
como los ojos de los pobres ahorcados.

Debo llorarte, Pueblo;
debo escribir tu nombre todos los días,
bebiendo café negro
y leyendo periódicos antiguos
en algún jardín abandonado.

Llorarte por mi encono—
por mis quejas ancladas en tu pecho—;
por esta frente atada a tu abandono,
y por este descuido del que hablo
pero que nada hago.

Empty religious folk
that don't know the strong pleas of love
when the poor carry them on their clothes
torn, smelling of earth and tired pain.
Empty religious folk, dry, even bitter,
closed off to our town's true suffering.

Oh, my Dark Town—
guitar broken over my heart—
we've lost it all and we are left
with our absent eyes
full of shards,
like the poor eyes of the hanged poor.

I should cry for you, Town;
I should write your name every day,
drinking black coffee
and reading ancient news
in some abandoned garden.

Cry for you, for my rancor—
for my complaints anchored in your chest—;
for this forehead tied to your abandon,
and for this neglect of which I speak
only to make and do nothing.

Aceptando el plato diario

El hombre aquel volvía al pueblo,
y comentaban los choferes amarrando sus uñas:
"Ese 'men' traerá su guitarra afilada".

Y todos se iban extendiendo por las aceras,
esparciendo sus malas palabras,
y deseando la mujer ajena.

En la oficina del correo las comadres chismeaban:
"¿Ve usted aquel?, ayer se llevó a Lena pa'la playa,
y dice Doña Luisa que es la tercera vez".

"Verdad, es",
afirma la vecina.

Los muchachos de escuela
lanzan carajos al barrendero torpe,
y el alcalde echa el brazo al jíbaro en la esquina.

Yo voy de paso;
llevo pantalón blanco y camisa planchada,
y a la gente le estorba y escupen a mi porte.

Mi gente es esto, aquello, y muchas otras cosas,
sopla ancha las verdades y es un poco envidiosa,
pero siendo mi gente, ¿cómo hacerle reproche?

Accepting the Daily Meal

That man was returning to town
and drivers commented, tying their fingernails:
"That guy will bring his sharpened guitar."

And all of them started covering the sidewalks,
tossing their bad words,
and desiring another man's wife.

At the post office midwives gossiped:
"See him over there? Yesterday he took Lena to the beach,
and Doña Luisa says it's the third time."

"It's true,"
the neighbor affirms.

The schoolboys
launch fucks at the clumsy street-sweeper
and, on the corner, the mayor throws his arm
    over the jíbaro's shoulder.

I'm just passing through;
wearing white pants and an ironed shirt,
and folks are bothered and they spit at my demeanor.

My people are this, that, and many other things,
they overinflate their truths and are a bit envious,
but being my people, how can I reproach?

Tormenta

Súbitamente el viento desespera
las casas apagadas de mi pueblo,
y la gente, casi sin sucesos,
sienten una rara sensación de vida.

Todos gritan ¡Tormenta!
Las calles y los cuerpos se confunden
en un rápido y turbado movimiento
de espaldas al silencio.

Indefensos, los árboles
quisieran escapar o esconderse en si mismos,
y no lográndolo
azotan fuerte, locos el espacio
que tanto tiempo
los tiene prisioneros.

Los gritos,
el miedo temblando en los ancianos,
los alaridos en los techos de zinc,
y las suplicas y rezos de las viejas
hace más amenazante el cielo.

Es el viento que huye **********************************.
un tropel de caballos entre espejos.

Aturdidas las calles no encuentran sus salidas.
La gente ha olvidado sus mensajes y cuentos.

Todos corremos y a ningún sitio vamos.
Estamos aturdidos y turbados,
pero hay algo de fiesta en el desorden.

(continued)

Storm

Suddenly the flaying wind inflames
my town's blown-out homes,
and almost uneventful people
feel a rare sense of life.

They all scream, Storm!
Streets with bodies confused
in a rapid and troubled movement
their backs turned on silence.

Defenseless, the trees
attempt to escape or crawl within themselves,
and when they can't,
hard and wild, they whip at space,
who, after all these years,
remains their jailor.

Screams,
fear shivering in elders,
barks heard on zinc roofs,
and the prayers of old women
broaden the harrowing sky.

It is the wind that flees ************************************.
a herd of horses racing through a field of mirrors.

Bewildered streets can't find their exits.
People have forgotten their messages and tales.

We all run and head nowhere.
We are stunned and distressed,
but there is something festive in our disorder.

(continued)

Si supieran los dueños de este pueblo
que he deseado callado
que el viento se arrebate y nos azote
y que solo nos deje
con árboles caídos y algo nuevo
que contarnos mañana uno al otro.

If only this town's owners knew
how I've silently wished
that the enraptured wind would thrash
and leave us with just
some fallen trees and something new
to tell each other in the morning.

Girl in the city

Llego con la mirada turbada de paisajes
y en mi barba traigo bosques y vientos.
Vengo grato de tierra, ligero de pesares,
y cuelgo mis dos chanclas sobre el retrato tuyo.

Si ofreces disculparte excuso, si me insultas descanso.
Voy y vengo de montes, soy de las soledades.
Mi corazón de plantas, mi alma plena de pájaros
espera como un árbol que extiendas tus ramajes.

Toma esta mi ternura de ásperas serranías
y enlázate ese cuerpo tan lleno de ciudades.
Quisiera que la blanca piel en que te sostienes
se llenase de obscuros bochornos en la tarde.

Muchacha en la ciudad

My gaze clouded by landscapes, I arrive.
In my beard: winds and forests.
Light of sorrows, full of earth, satisfied;
my two sandals above your portrait rest.

You insult, I halt; apologize, I'll excuse,
come and go from hills, being of solitudes.
My heart of plants, my soul with birds profuse,
awaits, as tree, your branches' plentitudes.

Take my tenderness of coarse mountain range
and weave that body with cities teeming.
I would love that white skin where you're sustained
darkened with embarrassments in evening.

Domingo sin iglesia

Mi brazo artificial,
echado sin reparos sobre un mueble,
puede reír igual que un zapato sin rumbos,
destruido,
tirado a lluvia y noches
en el patio de entonces.

Comprendo su ironía
y he pensado
en viejos almanaques,
en toallas obscuras,
en vapores de incienso
cuando monjas
pasan bajo el calor de mi ventana.

…Y es que mi brazo artificial
                    comprende —
tiene ese don supremo de reírse
cuando piensa en el cura y las señoras viejas
que alzan su rabia y destrozan púlpitos
cuando ven pocos pecadores.

Churchless Sunday

My artificial arm,
carelessly tossed on some couch,
can laugh like an aimless shoe,
destroyed,
thrown to nights and rain
in what was once my yard.

I understand its irony
and have thought
of old almanacs,
of dark towels,
of whiffs of incense
when nuns
pass beneath my window's warmth.

…You see my artificial arm
                    understands—
it has that supreme ability to laugh
when it thinks of the priest and old women
that raise their rage and destroy pulpits
if they see too few sinners.

Historia para otra historia

A Francisco Santiago del Río

Añasco tiene dos angostas puertas:
una que mira a lo pasado,
otra que mira a lo mismo de siempre.

Hace años—
cuando la primavera
todavía guardaba sus harapos—
andando por los bosques
él descubrió otra puerta.

Diferente,
bien escondida,
parecida a esas sorpresas halladas en los cuentos,
su presencia lo llenó de historias.

Ha conocido bien las estaciones;
lleva polvo
que haría crecer las plantas de otras tierras;
hay quienes lo confunden con sus sueños.

Si algún día, compueblano quieto,
descubres o te forjas esas puertas,
no te detengas,
crúzala.
Ábrele por favor otra salida
a nuestro obscuro pueblo.

Story for Another History
For Francisco Santiago del Río

Añasco has two narrow doors:
one that gazes at what's past,
another that watches the same old forever.

Years ago—
when spring
still stored its rags—
wandering through forests
he discovered another door.

Different,
quite hidden,
like a surprise found in stories,
its presence full of histories.

It's clearly familiar with the seasons,
full of dust
where plants from other lands would thrive;
some confuse it with their dreams.

If someday, peaceful neighbor,
you discover them or forge your own,
don't stop,
cross the threshold.
Please open another way
for our dark town.

La espera

El trópico,
con sudor y moscas,
entra a mi casa de campo.

Afuera el tiempo de la lluvia,
empujado por el viento negro,
me ensombrece un poco.

Discuten los relámpagos y el cielo...

Serán acaso las tres de la tarde
y en un rincón la siesta
está enredándose en mi flojo gato.

La espero nervioso.
¡Si llegase antes que la lluvia!

Mientras tanto la esperanza reza
y la música anda por la casa.

De no llegar me voy a caminar bajo la lluvia.

Y si acude,
¡ay!, si entra
a mi casa de campo y de poemas
voy a querer que llueva por cuarenta días.

The Wait

The tropics,
with sweat and flies,
enter my country home.

Outside, the rainy season,
pushed by the black wind,
somewhat casts me in shadows.

Lightning and sky bicker...

It must be three in the afternoon
and in a corner the midday nap
tangles with my detached cat.

Nervously, I wait for her.
If only she'd come before the storm!

Meanwhile hope prays
and music roams the house.

If she doesn't show, I'll go for a walk in the rain.

And if she arrives,
oh!, if she wanders
into my home of country fields and poems,
I'll pray it pours for forty days.

Jíbara que vio ciudad

La mujer arde y goza en su apretada falda.

La ve pasar viajera el hombre del sombrero
y no encuentra su adiós;
pero la sufre cerca y quisiera decir:
"Todavía la recuerdo bajo aquel flamboyán
y el río corriendo abajo.

Había muchos senderos en los cañaverales
y la yerba era alta y cosquillosa".

Mientras los hombres charlan,
la mujer ha pasado en su apretada falda
y no deja su adiós el hombre del sombrero.

"Quien sabe,
tal vez haya olvidado.

Eso sucede siempre —
cuando alguien se llena de ciudad
y vuelve al campo".

Jíbara That Saw City

The woman enflames and enjoys in her tight skirt.

The man in the hat sees her pass, a traveler,
and unsuccessfully searches for his goodbye;
but suffers her closeness and wants to say:
"I still remember her beneath the flamboyán
with the river flowing downstream.

There were many trails among the cane fields
and the grass was ticklish and tall."

While the men are talking,
the woman has passed in her tight skirt
and the man in the hat leaves no goodbye.

"Who knows,
perhaps she has forgotten.

That always happens—
when someone gets full of city
and comes back to the country."

Entonces

Ya no podré robar toronjas,
ni atropellar el río,
ni jugar con mi prima entre la yerba,
o molestar las viejas
que aun usan colorete a los ochenta.

No bajaré más dulces a pedradas,
ni cantaré en la calle,
ni jugaré a los dados en un arco
de haraposos muchachos sin escuela.

Dejaré quieto los nidos de gallinas,
no asaltaré a escondidas la merienda,
ni cargaré Los Reyes en parrandas.

En cambio seré calvo, rechoncho;
con corbata y sombrero pasearé por el parque,
sin mi honda, mis topos,
mi chavo con dos caras,
mi pantalón con parchos,
y aquella boca de melao y manteca
que fue la mejor fuente de mi risa.

Then

I'll no longer get to steal grapefruit,
nor run over the river,
nor play with my cousin in the tall grass,
or bother old women
who still wear blush at eighty.

I'll no longer knock down candy with stones,
nor sing in the street,
nor play with dice in an arc
of raggedy, school-deprived boys.

I'll leave the chickens' nests alone,
I will not stealthily snatch lunches,
nor carry the Wise Men in parrandas.

In return, I'll be bald, fat;
in a hat and tie I'll stroll through the park,
without my sling, my spinning tops,
my two-headed quarter,
my patched pants,
and that mouth of molasses and lard
that was the best source of my laughter.

1963
SELECCIÓN POÉTICA

FECHA DESCONOCIDAS

1963
SELECTED POEMS

UNKNOWN DATES

Ahí un dulce silencio
de momentos ~~no~~ rotos
entre tú y yo, Atasco mío.

A veces se sacude
la aurora sobre tus espalda
y deja un millar de
estrellas durmiendo escondidas
en tus sendas azules,
blancas, verde-azules.

Ahí un recuerdo

Thursday, FEBRUARY 7

38th Day—327 days to come

Ahí, un dulce silencio
de momentos rotos
entre tú y yo, Añasco mío.

A veces se sacude
la aurora sobre tu espalda
y deja un millar de
estrellas durmiendo escondidas
entre tus sendas azules,
blancas, verde-azules.

Ahí, un recuerdo.

Thursday, FEBRUARY 7

38th Day—327 days to come

There, a sweet silence
of moments broken
between us, my Añasco.

Sometimes the dawn
brushes off on your back
and leaves a thousand
stars slumbering hidden
between your blue,
white, and blue-green paths.

There, a memory.

Monday, FEBRUARY 18

49th Day--316 days to come

El ven que trajo dos
de cabeza en el río

Monday, FEBRUARY 18

49th Day—316 days to come

El resquebrajo claro
de la luz en el río

Monday, FEBRUARY 18

49th Day—316 days to come

The clear crack
of light in the river

Que irremediable d p habe
perdido

Y tengo algo que tuvo
todas nunca —

ya se resuelve el que
como abeja sin miel
en no alcanzar los
altos ramajes de la
noche.

Thursday, JUNE 27

178th Day—187 days to come

Que irremediable algo habré perdido
y tengo algo que tú no
tendrás nunca

ya se revuelve el alma
como abeja sin mieles
en no alcanzar los
altos ramajes de la
noche

Thursday, JUNE 27

178th Day—187 days to come

What irremediable something I must have lost
and I have something that you
will never have

already the soul stirs
like a bee without honeys
for it cannot reach the
night's
high branches

El mar for aburrido

los frutos del mar vienen
de adentro
los de la tierra puede
uno madurarlos poco a
poco al toque de las
manos

Friday, JUNE 28

179th Day—186 days to come

El mar por aburrido

los frutos del mar vienen
de adentro
los de la tierra puede
uno madurarlos poco a
poco al toque de las
manos

Friday, JUNE 28

179th Day—186 days to come

The sea out of boredom

the fruits of the sea come
from within
those of the earth
one can ripen little by
little to the touch
of hands

Campo Muerto, tiempo seco,
la techumbre de la historia

Monday, JULY 22

203rd Day—16 days to come

Campo muerto, tiempo seco,
la herrumbre de la historia

Monday, JULY 22

203rd Day—16 days to come

Dead fields, dry season,
the rust of history

NADA PIERDES, CABALLO VIEJO
(FAENA DE REMEDIOS)

SELECCIÓN POÉTICA, 1989

YOU LOSE NOTHING,
OLD HORSE (REMEDY WORK)

SELECTED POEMS, 1989

Noción de lo imposible

Llegó una tarde
yo brillaba zapatos
era tan indeciblemente hermosa
que tuve lástima de mí

Me observó como un bajo crepúsculo
y zozobrando pensé en amaneceres
qué orillas qué tierras me abrumaron
era algo más allá de mi vida

Recelé entonces que el cielo era imposible
y nunca fui tan lastimado

(1986)

A Sense of the Impossible

One afternoon
I was shining shoes
she was so unspeakably stunning
I took pity on myself

She observed me like a low dusk
and foundering I thought of dawns
what shores what lands overtook me
it was something beyond my life

I feared, then and there, that the sky was impossible
and my wound was never deeper

(1986)

Canción de amor

Me levanté temprano
era azul la mañana,
pero mi amor había salido antes
ya había atravesado los umbrales del Alba

Canción de amor (Pápago)

todos los días
viajo la finca al campo abierto
y voy pensándote

en las tardes
en las tranquilas tardes
que pacen las colinas
te espero sin premura

toda en mí estás
como una agua redonda y contenida
aunque ya tus pisadas
han borrado la lluvia

(1964)

Love Song

I woke up early
the morning was blue,
but my love had left already
had crossed the threshold of Dawn

Love Song (Pápago)

every day
I cross the farm to the open fields
and along the way I think of you

in the afternoons
in the quiet afternoons
that graze the hills
I patiently wait for you

you are all in me
like a round and contained water
even though your footsteps
already erased the rain

(1964)

Mi vecino

Yo no odio a mi vecino
pero no me agrada la forma en que me mira a mi perro

Antes mis gallinas evitaban el monte
y tenían sus miradas el color de la tierra seca

Ahora los tomates logran caerse y las gallinas
cantan unas canciones como la risa de la hierba joven
que le enseñaron los pájaros cuando estábamos ausentes

Pero me mira mi vecino como mira a mi perro

(1960)

My Neighbor

I don't hate my neighbor
but I dislike how he looks at my dog

It used to be my chickens avoided the mountains
and had the color of dry earth in their stares

Now the tomatoes successfully drop and the chickens
sing a few songs with the laughter of young grass
which they learned from the birds while we were out of town

But my neighbor looks at me like he looks at my dog

(1960)

Vocación

Aporte usted
escriba pinte moldee
cante la Patria
diga su verdad a los cuatro vientos
y tendrá usted derecho
a que le nieguen todo…
salvo un lugar entre paredes

(1978)

Vocation

Contribute
write paint shape
sing to the Patria
shout your truth from the rooftops
and you will have the right
to be denied everything...
except a room with padded walls

(1978)

Pensando repasando

Mañana evaluaremos este día
y tal vez no nos sobre
ni la izquierda del cero

Aunque es posible
que nos reste una deuda
pero bien bien seguro
una duda
una insondable duda

Porque una deuda
se le carga a cualquiera hasta más luego
pero esta duda
la arrastraremos siempre hasta la muerte
y sabe Dios…

(1986)

Thinking and Reviewing

Tomorrow we shall evaluate this day
and perhaps nothing will be left
not even the left of zero

Although it is possible
we have a left-over debt
but for definitely sure
a doubt
an unfathomable doubt

Because a debt
can be unburdened on someone later
but this doubt
we will carry it always until death
and even then, God only knows…

(1986)

CUADERNO DE
TIERRA Y HOMBRE

(1956–1973)

...porque estoy triste y viajo,
y conozco la tierra y estoy triste.

Pablo Neruda

JOURNAL OF
EARTH AND MAN

(1956–1973)

…because I am sad and travel,
and know the earth and am sad.

Pablo Neruda

I

LA TIERRA Y SUS ESTACIONES

I

THE EARTH AND ITS SEASONS

Humatas

...Y tu mirada verde para todos los días
(cuando se abrían tus manos de pájaros y flores
y las cabras mordían los gritos del rocío).

Entonces tú tendrías doce años, Humatas,
y mis pies rastreaban tus veredas y ríos
y tus jaldas mis uñas llenaban de colores.

Cariño aquel y campo
donde el hicaco hablaba un idioma tan puro
y el maíz entregaba sus amarillos dientes
en destronada risa sobre jíbaras faldas.

(Será larga esta seca, pensaban los compadres,
y bebían café prieto en livianas jatacas).
Ay de mí y tu recuerdo —
tus noches de linternas y apacibles hamacas
bajo la tibia luna pariéndose de gallos.

Era saberte así. Barrio de hondos rumores,
con olor a fogones durmiéndose en cenizas
y perfume de frutos reventando en los ramos.

Mientras en la espesura un pájaro de gárgaras
desvestía al cafetal su poderío de granos.

Era saberte así,
cuando entraban los pasos de espíritus nocturnos —
la aventura y la noche cogidas de las manos —
por las entonces claras rendijas de mi alma.

Y ahora que te pienso después de tantas siembras,
¿sigues, Humatas, siendo un canasto de cuentos
bajo el quinqué ahumado y el techo sin tablado?

(continued)

Humatas

... And your gaze, green for all time,
(when your bird and flower hands would open
and goats would bite the dew's screams).

Then you'd be about twelve, Humatas,
and my feet would track your paths and rivers
and your mountains' laps would paint my nails.

That tender touch, those fields
where the hicaco spoke a language so pure
and corn released its yellow teeth
in dethroned laughter onto jíbara skirts.

(This drought will be long, thought the compadres,
drinking their dark-skinned coffee in light jatacas).
Alas, my mind and your memory—
your nights full of lanterns and peaceful hammocks
under a warm moon brimming with roosters.

It was to know you like that. Barrio of deep whispers,
with a smell of hearths dozing off into ashes
and fruits' perfume bursting on branches.

While in the thickness a gargling bird
disrobed the coffee field of its mighty grain.

It was to know you like that,
when the entering steps of nocturnal spirits passed—
adventure and night holding hands—
through the then clear slits in my soul.

And now that I think of you after so many harvests,
are you still, Humatas, a basket of stories
under the smoky quinqué and the unpaneled roof?

(continued)

¿Qué de aquellos caminos de lodo o blando polvo,
cuando el mechón hablaba a los enamorados
que regresaban tarde de bailes o rosarios?

Antiguo, casi ido, Barrio,
por donde yo corría con mis jíbaros gustos
y las manos preñadas de pajuil y guayabos.

¿Acaso olvidaría el grito del vecino
que desde algunas millas — de montaña a montaña —
gritaba que la vaca se salió del cercado?

Humatas — viejo Barrio
que sabes de mi herencia y de mis pies descalzos
trepando palo'e panas y saltando barrancos.

Sólo un ratito déjame recordar tu cariño:
cuando me conociste tan libre por tus montes
alborotando avispas y cantando aguinaldos.

Sólo un ratito, Humatas —
Barrio que ahora me tienes
tan lejos de tu seno y de ciudad amargo.

San Mateo College (1956)

What happened to those paths of clay or yielding dust,
when the lock of hair murmured to those in love
as they returned late from dances or rosary prayers?

Ancient, almost gone, Barrio,
where I ran with my jíbaro tastes,
my hands pregnant with pajuil and guayabos.

Could I ever forget the neighbor's call
who, some miles away—from mountain to mountain—,
screamed that the cow broke past the fence?

Humatas—old Barrio
that knows of my inheritance and my naked soles
climbing pana trees and leaping ravines.

Only a little while, let me remember you were tender:
when you knew me in my mountainous freedom,
rampaging wasps' nests and singing aguinaldos.

Only a little while, Humatas—
Barrio who now has me
so far from your breast and bitter with city.

San Mateo College (1956)

Añoranza

¡Aquello sí era amor!...
La tierra seca,
el caballo embriagado en las crines del aire,
y ya cerca el batey me enseñaba la cara,
¡Aquello sí era amor!...

Por el aire bogaban palabras sueltas,
la voz de la guitarra saltaba entre las mozas
y el güiro como un viejo de risa se arqueaba.

Era diciembre antiguo hirviendo sus pasteles
con su batey de seis y aguinaldo de Reyes,
y yo con mi caballo sobre la tierra seca.
¡Aquello sí era amor!...

(1957)

Yearning

Now that was love!
The dry earth,
the horse drunkenly grazing in the air's mane,
and already arriving the batey showed me its face,
Now that was love! ...

Through the air rowed loose words,
the guitar's voice pranced among girls,
and the güiro like an old man arched with laughter.

It was ancient December boiling pasteles
with its batey for six and Three Kings aguinaldo,
as I rode my horse across the dry earth.
Now that was love! ...

(1957)

Este Yo rizoma

Si no admitiese la grave desventura de los hombres
me gustaría llevar el rostro sucio y la camisa rota.

Yo encontraría en los nudos de la caña y el carbón de los hornos
la fuerza que he perdido por caminos extraños.

Sería dulce de fango y contento en la siembra;
casi de sol y lluvia anhelaría una hembra
que tuviese caderas tan verdes como Añasco.

Y así, mientras contemple en mis tardes de campo
mi pequeña fortuna de surcos y de tallos,
ir cosiendo en la hamaca,
con olor a café y la pereza de fogones tibios,
mi coraza de cáscaras de jíbaro contento.

This Rhizome I

If I didn't admit man's grave misfortune,
I'd love to wear a dirty face and a ripped shirt.

In sugarcane knots and the charcoal of stoves,
I'd find the strength I lost on strange roads.

I'd be sweet with mud and joyous when sowing;
I'd wish for a woman almost made of sun and rain
whose hips could rival Añasco's green.

And thus, while contemplating my country evenings,
my small fortune of grooves and stems,
I'd start sewing in the hammock,
the air thick with coffee and the sloth of warm hearths,
my breastplate of contented jíbaro rinds.

Carta a la hermana

Desde la otra ciudad
Tercer día otoñal del 59

Querida hermana:

Si vas al campo el viernes no lleves, por favor, a tu amiga de siempre.

Sigue entonces el camino rojo en la tarde y rojo en la mañana y con bastantes charcos de luceros sangrantes en las noches con un poco de sol. Desde luego, ha llovido estos días y sentirás blanda la tierra y mojada la piel de los helechos, mas si te cubres con un poco de barro, gózalo hasta la quebrada próxima que baja cantando y que pronto dará un agua como el color de algunos claros de bosques y suave y rápida como las mejillas de los niños alegres.

Corta ahora por la vereda de los mameyes y aguza el oído a los pájaros. Notarás lo ruidosos que son. Siempre suenan así por esos montes.

Ahora busca a tu izquierda. Verás el cafetal inclinado como baja corriendo hasta un cierto ruido sordo allá en el fondo. No creas, es sólo un pequeño río, que, según tío Peyo, baja desde los lindes de la gran finca de doña Concha.

Sigue caminando y pronto llegarás a una cerca de mayas y ahí es donde comienzan las huellas y el sudor de la familia.

Recuerda, hay dos caminos: uno que trepa al saludo de doña Toñita; el otro sube hasta la sonrisa de tía. Debes seguir cualquiera—el campo siempre lleva a buenos sitios. Sin embargo, el segundo te parecerá más gastado, ya que tío Peyo tiene alma de güiro y parece un árbol en el viento cuando tiene la casa llena y el cuatro y las maracas se desesperan y desesperan.

Es posible que no estén los muchachos—ellos trabajan hasta que el sol se arruina—, pero te recibirán el abrazo de tía y el olor a café en su cocina. No olvides que tienen una nevera de gas y que siempre hay cervezas en ella. Pierde cuidado que a tía también le gustan.

Bien, aquí te dejo, puesto que ya tienes tu hamaca entre árboles, tu cuerpo en la brisa más pura y tu voz en el monte. Te sería muy fácil seguir viviendo.

Te piensa dulcemente,
Tu hermano

Letter to the Sister

From the other city
Third autumnal day of '59

Dear sister:

If you go to the countryside on Friday, please, don't take your usual friend.

Then follow the path that is red in the afternoon and red in the morning and has plenty of puddles full of stars bleeding at night with a bit of sun. Of course, it has rained these days and you'll feel the earth is soft and the skin of the ferns wet, especially if you cover yourself with a little mud, enjoy it up until the next stream that comes down singing and will soon sprout a water like the color of certain forest clearings and smooth and swift like the cheeks of cheerful children.

Now take the shortcut down the mamey path and prick up your ears to hear the birds. You will notice how noisy they are. They always sound like that in these mountains.

Now, look left. You'll see the coffee plantation sloping as it drops fast until it reaches a certain deaf sound there at the bottom. Don't worry, it's only a small river, that, according to tío Peyo, flows down from the borders of doña Concha's big farm.

Keep walking and soon you'll reach a mesh fence and that's where the family's footprints and sweat start.

Remember, there are two paths: one that climbs up to doña Toñita's greeting; the other that climbs until it reaches tía's smile. You should follow either one — the countryside always leads to good places. Still, the second path will seem the most worn, since tío Peyo has a güiro soul and looks like a tree in the wind when he has a full house and the cuatro and the maracas get more and more desperate.

It's possible the boys aren't home — they work until the sun is ruined —, but you'll be greeted by tía's embrace and the smell of coffee in the kitchen. Don't forget, their gas fridge is always stocked with beers. Don't hold back, tía also likes to have a few.

Well, I'll be taking my leave of you, since you've already hung your hammock in the trees, your body is in the purest breeze and your voice is in the mountains. To go on living will come easy.

I send you sweet thoughts,
Your brother

Mañana lluviosa

En la mañana que llueve
los carreteros cruzan dulcemente mi estancia
y la vecina de todos arde amorosamente con su amante.

Estoy pensando cómo bajarán de crecidas
las quebradas altas a los ríos.

La abierta mano de la clara lluvia barre los tejados.
Qué fácil es ser vago en estos días
y tener una mujer en la cocina.

Pobrecitas gallinas que se lanzaron aplastadas del árbol
y entran a sacudirse bajo la casa.

Seré bueno y bajaré con el maíz;
luego subiré con alguna lluvia y tomaré la sopa,
mientras de afuerta me llegará la tierra—
mojada y honda, olorosa y desnuda—
y su recuerdo como un ancho aguacero.

(1960)

Rainy Morning

Through the morning rain,
the waggoners sweetly cross my stay
and our common neighbor with her lover tenderly stings and burns.

I'm thinking how they'll torrentially descend,
the high streams down into rivers.

Clear rain's open hand sweeps the shingles.
These days, it's so easy to be lazy
and have a woman in the kitchen.

Poor dears, the chickens launched themselves flat from the tree
and head to shake off beneath the house.

I'll be good and come down with the corn;
later I'll rise with some rain and eat soup,
while the earth reaches through the open door—
wet and deep, fragrant and bare—
its memory like a vast downpour.

(1960)

Elegía mayor a la tierra

Tu también eres, Pitirre,
en este suelo un extraño.

Al pasado, porque de él me me llegaron
las fuerzas fundamentales para trabajar
este presente.

Era nuestra la tierra,
y sobre ella
comíamos el casabe que daba para todos,
porque no esperábamos extraños
y nuestras yucas eran suficientes.

Interminable cantaba el bosque sin alambres
y a orillas del Guaorabo
el tiempo con sus claras sombras se tendía.

El aguacero se movía prendido al aire
y en la noche, el misterio recóndito de oscuro vegetal
rodaba el agua.

¿Recuerdas, Urayoán?
Imponía la mañana su página de árboles
lanzándolos sus débiles azúcares,
sus espesos ramajes musicales,
cuando en los rutilantes ojos del rocío
intuiste el agua como un signo:
"Llenos los ríos la muerte puede ser de agua."

(continued)

Major Elegy to the Earth

You, Pitirre, are also
a stranger to this land.

To the past, because he brought me
the fundamental strength to work on
this present.

The land was ours,
and on her
we ate casabe and there was enough for all,
since we never expected strangers
and our yucas were sufficient.

The forest free of barbwire sang interminably
and on Guaorabo's shores
time with its clear shadows hung on the clothesline.

The downpour moved, trailing the air,
and in the night, the recondite mystery of a dark vegetable
circled the water.

Remember, Urayoán?
Morning imposed its page of trees,
tossing us its weak sugars,
its musically dense branches,
when in dawn's glittering eyes
you intuited the water like a sign:
"With the rivers full death might break water."

(continued)

2

Por eso ten cuidado, Celeste,
no te acerques al borde de la charca,
esa humedad oliente te hace daño.

Es mejor que des vueltas,
da vueltas en tu jardín con flores numeradas;
da vueltas y recoge las grandes hojas
de negra clorofila y nervios acerados
y entenderás tu cielo de neón y perfectas estrellas
donde nos llegan los extraños como duendes
y tumban nuestras cercas
para sembrar enormes árboles de concreto y metales.

Por las costuras del día—antes espigas en mi tala—
observad a los pájaros de oxidados plumajes
que en aleteo metálico desnudan a la tierra.

3

Oh, Hermano, ésta es la gruesa noche de las aberraciones.

Ya se resuelve el alma como abeja sin mieles
en no alcanzar los áridos panales del recuerdo
Yo aquí tendido, sin tierra ni canciones,
allá sueñan mis niños con sus manos pequeñas.

Mientras lejanos perros llegan oscuramente
y van acumulando poco a poco sus fauces.
¡Oh extraña Tierra mía,
te encaminabas a un alba de sucias claridades!

(continued)

2

So be careful, Celeste,
don't approach the pool's edge,
that foul humidity is harmful.

It's best you turn around, you walk in circles
in your garden of enumerated flowers;
spin around and around and gather large leaves
of black chlorophyll and steely nerves
and you'll understand your neon sky and perfect stars
where strangers arrive like duendes
and knock down our fences
to plant enormous metal and concrete trees.

Through the day's seams—once spikes in my felling—
observe the birds with their oxidated plumage
that with metallic flapping strip the earth.

3

Oh, Brother, this is the thick night of aberrations.

The soul already finds a way, like a bee without honeys
when it can't reach the arid honeycombs of memory.
Here I am, stretched out to dry, without land or songs,
over there my children dream of their small hands.

While distant dogs arrive darkly
and little by little accrue their maws.
¡Oh my strange Earth,
you headed toward a dawn of dirty clarities!

(continued)

4

Cuando sólo eras río,
río pequeño donde el incierto fruto se alargaba,
entonces,
entonces era clara primavera.

Mas ya ves,
aquí no hay ríos para bañar mis días,
aunque llueve continuamente
y corrientes extrañas se cuelan por las rendijas del campo
y barren nuestras siembras.

Son como ríos que corren sin turbarse,
pero yo sólo amo ríos perdidos;
porque toda agua recta es cauce preso
por donde van las lluvias a la venta.

5

¿Habita Mabo el Grande tu amable fortaleza
cuando el hambre de paso
y pájaros devoradores lanzados de otras ramas
entran en nuestra huerta y asaltan sus cosechas?

¿Por qué odias el recuerdo de los anchos crepúsculos
allá cuando el viento y la lluvia tumbaban nuestras puertas
y ornaban nuestros setos los paisajes en luz de los relámpagos?

Bajaba la quebrada rebasando su roída estatura
y en hálitos de frío se estremecían los frutos en el monte.
Después el día explotando sus júbilos secretos:
astillaban los pájaros la callada espesura
y la yerba y la rama en su hinchazón de agua
dilataban el ánimo que trajo el aguacero.

(continued)

4

When you were only river,
small river where uncertain fruit lengthened,
then,
then it was bright spring.

But now you see,
here there are no rivers to bathe my days,
although it rains steadily
and strange currents slip in through field slits
and sweep away our harvests.

They are like rivers with unmuddied flow,
but I only love lost rivers;
for all unswerving water is a gully jailed
where rains are bought and sold.

5

Does Mabo the Great live in your amiable fortress
when, passing through, hunger
and devouring birds taking flight from other branches
enter our orchard and attack its crops?

Why do you hate the memory of expansive dusks
back when wind and rain knocked down our doors
and lighting landscapes adorned our hedges?

The stream came down overflowing its gnawed stature
and in cold halite breaths the mountain fruit shivered.
As the day went on erupting its secret jubilees:
the birds splintered the quiet thicket,
as grass and branch with their water bellies
distended the mood brought on by downpour.

(continued)

Así cantaba el tiempo sus órdenes celestes
cuando nuestra era la sangre doblada en los bateyes;
porque nosotros mismos nos matábamos,
y nosotros mismos nos matábamos,
y nosotros mismos nos rezábamos,
y nosotros mismos nos sembrábamos
en nuestra propia tierra.

Pero nada nos queda sin líquenes extraños.
Somos frutos anómalos de un árbol que enloquece
buscando un sobresalto de antigua primavera.

Por eso es mi presencia como una amarga cáscara
de cosas desprovistas de los días que recuerdo.

Y algo ha de sucederme si he de seguir viviendo:
algo como una muerte de rotos ruiseñores
que han perdido sus últimos clamores musicales.

Y que sigan los árboles cayendo,
emigrando los pájaros sus voces
o plegando sus alas mansamente.

Que prosigan las noches homicidas
y columpiando el mar extrañas huestes.

Ya nos llegan los jóvenes que aran leve la tierra
para legar al mundo árboles sin raíces.

(continued)

That's how time sang its celestial orders,
when ours was the blood folded into bateyes;
because we ourselves killed ourselves and each other,
and we ourselves prayed for ourselves and each other,
and we ourselves sowed ourselves and each other
on our own land.

But nothing we had is left without strange lichens.
We are anomalous fruits of a tree gone mad
seeking a frightful leap of ancient spring.

This is why my presence is like a bitter peel
of things wrung empty of the days I remember.

And something will befall me if I'm to keep living:
something like a death of mangled mockingbirds
that have lost their last musical clamors.

And may trees continue falling,
birds continue migrating their voices
and folding their wings tamely.

May homicidal nights persist
and may the sea still swing strange troops.

Young men are now arriving who plow the earth too lightly,
in their wills leaving the world with rootless trees.

(continued)

6

Te hablo de consecuencias que no doblan tus hombros,
pues afilas tus dedos y señalas mi barro
y tus pies van negando su barranco de huellas.

(Del pasado no cuidas ni tu campo de muertos.)
Y siento que la sangre se ha anudado en tus venas.

Ya que la misma piedra conserva su pasado:
ved sus caries oscuras y su musgo latente.

7

No te sostiene ahora tu raíz aborigen.
Te ha surcando el recuerdo de un mal año de siembras.
Por eso, Hermano mío, únicamente grietas somos de aquellos días,
los renegados días,
por donde iba el buen hombre de la orilla del río,
del recio corazón como las aguas girando bajo la tempestad.

Y también el leñero del hacha centelleante
y el llano carretero de la piel de bagazo
con la noche y el día grabado en cicatrices;
los cansados y enérgicos, diría,
parte integral en el destino de mi gente.

Aquello es para ti toda una tarde lánguida
con lluvias en los montes, fango por el camino
y pies podridos en la tierra blanda.

Razón por la que juzgas soy una rama absurda
que va y viene meciéndose del sueño a la vigilia
y nada te produce, ni te alegra, ni te orilla palabras amorosas.

(continued)

6

I'm speaking of consequences that don't hunch your shoulders,
for you sharpen your fingers and point to my clay
and your feet go negating the ravine of their tracks.

(And the past? You don't even trim your yard full of graves.)
And I sense that blood is now knotted in your veins.

Now that the same stone preserves its past:
see its dark cavities and its latent moss.

7

Now your aboriginal root won't uphold you.
You've been furrowed by the memory of a bad harvest.
This is why, Brother, we are but fissures of those days,
those renegade, those renounced days,
tread by that good man from the riverbank,
whose fresh and tough heart whirled like waters in a tempest.

And also the lumberjack of the scintillating ax
and the shallow wagoner with bagasse skin
with night and day engraved in scars;
the tired and energetic days, I'd say,
are an integral part of my people's fate.

For you, that is all just one languid afternoon
with rains on the mountainsides, mud on the road,
and feet rotted in the slush earth.

Which is why you swear I'm an absurd branch
that comes and goes swinging from dream to wake
and you feel nothing, nothing gives you joy, nor docks loving words
    on your shore.

(continued)

8

(Ven, María,
tus largas trenzas
recórtalas a tiempo.

¡María,
que ya cabalga el sol y te azota la piel!

¡Las lloviznas, María!
¡Corre, María,
que viene el aguacero y te enlodas los pies!

¡El sereno, María!

¿Ves a Celeste de las suaves piernas?
Ahí está la gracia.

Cubre tus pies, María, y descubre tus muslos.

Hay que aprender, querida:
has de quebrar la rama para lograr el fruto.)

(continued)

8

(Come, María,
your long braids,
cut them in time.

María!
The sun already rides and whips your skin!

The rain showers, María!
Run, María,
the downpour is coming! And your feet are getting muddy!

The sereno, María!

Do you see Celeste of the smooth legs?
That is grace.

Cover your feet, María, and uncover your thighs.

You must learn, dear:
you must break the branch to reach the fruit.)

(continued)

9

Hoy
por tus caminos de verano
transitan los grandes canallas del espíritu
que arman sus existencias con números y números,
y en un árbol caído yace el viento
que meció mis primeras ilusiones.

Todo en mí se debate callada y mansamente,
aunque a veces me digo:
Si la Tierra no fuese dócil,
si de momento levantase su tierra
con árboles y pájaros y frutos,
como los terremotos y tornados,
como los huracanes,
hasta arruinar los techos del paisaje.

Si la Tierra obligase a sus esporas
a penetrar el tiempo de los frutos,
para que sufran árboles sin promesas,
de sexos alterados y sin pájaros
en parajes de amor elaborado.

Pero todo se mece mansamente
y estoy tan destruido
que ya acaso ni entristecerme puedo.

Sólo añoro un lugar callado y hondo
para ir acostumbrándome al silencio.

(continued)

9

Today
down your summer roads
ride the greatest villains of the spirit
who arm their existences with numbers and numbers,
and in a fallen tree sleeps the wind
that pushed me, swinging my first flights.

Everything within me quiet and tamely debates itself,
although I sometimes think:
What if the Earth were not so docile,
what if it suddenly lifted its earth
with trees and birds and fruit,
like earthquakes and tornados,
like hurricanes,
ruining the roofs of this vision.

What if the Earth forced its spores
to penetrate the fruits' seasons,
to cause suffering in trees without promises,
with altered sexes and without birds
in parajes of elaborated and elaborate love.

But everything swings tamely
and I am so destroyed
that I can barely become sad.

I only yearn for a quiet and deep place
where I can grow accustomed to silence.

(continued)

Ven Guaybaná—
ven capeador de fieras tempestades—,
barre con mis palabras de este día;
llévate el dulce nombre que menciono
y que no me responde,
porque entiende
que yo también padezco de liviano
y ando sobre las cosas levemente.

Y es que para ser heroico,
para alcanzar espacios,
primeramente hay que nacer bien hondo,
como la tierra misma,
y surgir lentamente, inquebrantable,
agrietando la inquina de la roca
hasta lograr el cielo del paisaje
e imponer nuestro imperio de follaje.

Si esto digo,
es porque las cosas hondas no se entregan
sino a ciertos impulsos más profundos.

Y no es amor el dedo que señala
sino lo mueve un cauce de ternura.

Un cauce inalienable como un río
siempre abierto a la sed de sus dominios.

Yo, por lo tanto, vivo al margen de la tierra.

Esa es la gran tristeza de la que yo te hablaba.

(1963)

10

Come Guaybaná—
come capeador of fierce tempests—,
sweep away my words belonging to this day;
take the sweet name on my lips
and that won't answer,
because it understands
I too suffer this condition called levity
and walk lightly across all things.

The thing is that to be heroic,
to reach spaces,
we must first be born in the deepest deep,
like the earth itself
and sprout slowly, unwavering,
cracking the anger in the rock
until we've wrestled a sky out of a landscape
and imposed our foliage empire.

If I say this,
it's because deep things don't surrender
except to certain deeper drives.

And there is no love in the finger that points
if not moved by the channel of a tender hand.

A riverbed as inalienable as a river
always open to the thirst of its dominions.

I, therefore, live on the fringes of the earth.

This is the great sadness that I mentioned.

(1963)

II

NARCISO EN VERANO

II

NARCISSUS IN SUMMER

Equilibrio

Los otros días llegaron los pájaros negros
que saben gritar
y asaltaron mi cosecha ya próxima.

Mi mujer, que tomaba el chocolate en el balcón,
fue quién los vio,
mientras escuchaba los ruidos navegar en la tarde.

Yo, que siempre ando por los montes,
no supe nada hasta que llegó la noche.

No quería ella preparar las perdices;
me decía que sus plumas eran suaves y hermosas,
y por eso los pájaros negros doblaban las espigas.

(1960)

Equilibrium

The other day arrived the black birds
who certainly can caw
and attacked my latest harvest.

It was my wife, drinking chocolate on the porch,
who saw them,
as she heard noises steering through the afternoon.

I, who am always on the side of some mountain,
knew nothing until nightfall.

She didn't want to cook the partridges;
she told me their feathers were soft and lovely
and that is why the black birds bent the spikes.

(1960)

Mireya

Tiene Mireya cosas que hacen gratos los días.

Para llegar a la quebrada cruza por detrás de mi casa
con pasos que hacen gritar las hojas, sin que el perro
le haga otro gesto que el olerla y seguirla.

Otras veces se desliza en mi finca
y exprime contra sus labios fuertes
las dulces chinas que gotean en diciembre,
o se lleva las guanábanas olorosas y espesas
que todos los años caen abiertamente sobre el camino.

Mireya vive en una casa roída que ya no grita bajo el sol caliente
y con patio rojísimo en las caídas de tardes.

La he visto bañarse en la lluvia;
sembrar flores cantando ruidosamente erizadas canciones.

Así, todos los días me encuentro con Mireya.
Ella tan cristalina y fuerte,
con ese familiar atrevimiento de hacer mi finca suya;
yo callado y firme,
corriendo dentro de mí.

(1960)

Mireya

Mireya does things that brighten the days.

She crosses behind my house to reach the creek
with steps that make the leaves scream, and the dog
does nothing but sniff and follow suit.

Other times she glides across my farm,
squeezing against her strong lips
the sweet oranges that drip in December,
or she takes the fragrantly thick guanábanas
that each year openly drop onto the road.

Mireya lives in a gnawed house that no longer wails
    under the scorching sun,
with a yard shockingly red from evening's slip-and-falls.

I've seen her shower in the rain;
plant flowers noisily singing bristled songs.

Just like that, I run into Mireya every day.
So crystalline and tough, there she is,
with that familiar daring to make my farm hers;
while I, stoic and strong,
run circles inside.

(1960)

Epanáfora del vacío

Después de la gran borrachera nocturna
vago calladamente bajo los altos árboles.

Las viejas cogedoras de café me observan sentenciosas,
con un ritmo temblón y chismoso.

Piensan que soy un torpe vago,
que me baño desnudo en el río,
y recibo una pensión del gobierno.

Como el tedio me invita,
vuelvo por tardes a la tienda cercana
y me emborracho viciosamente.

Luego por las mañanas un poco frías
vago otra vez bajo los altos árboles,
sin nada que decir, ni pensar, ni esperar...

Anaphora of Emptiness

After the great nocturnal binge
I roam quietly under the tall trees.

Old women gathering coffee observe me sententiously
with a trembling and gossipy rhythm.

They think I'm a clumsy, lazy drunk,
who skinny-dips in rivers,
and receives a government pension.

Since boredom's paying,
each afternoon I return to the nearby store
and viciously drink.

Later on slightly cold mornings
I roam again under the tall trees,
with nothing to say, or think, or expect...

Lessueste de lo posible

A veces no quisiera madrugar con mi señora,
y levantándome temprano
me deslizo calladamente entre la neblina de los caminos,
evitando siempre el rumor mañanero de algunas casas.

Así vuelvo a lugares
que me detienen a pensar en algunas ocasiones sin amor...

Y me pregunto si es posible que un día
alguien cruce el portón de nuestra casa
y todo se vuelva de espaldas...

De un antro de modorra
puede surgir un arpa,
o un niño sorprendente, inverosímil,
como un lirio brotando de metales quebrados,
o un flamboyán ardiendo den el más crudo invierno.

Y porque he meditado sobre ello regresaré contento a casa
y tomaré café sentado en la escalera sur,
frente a la hortaliza que destrozaron los perros anoche.

(1960)

East of Possible

Sometimes I don't want to rise with my woman
and getting up early
I creep out quietly through the road mist,
always avoiding the first rustlings of certain houses.

That's how I end up returning to places
that make me stop and think on loveless days...

And I ask myself is it possible that sometime
someone might cross the gate to our house,
flipping everything on its back...

A harp might step out
from any drowsy bar,
or a surprising, implausible child
like a lily blooming out of cracked metals,
or a flamboyán burning in the rawest winter.

And because I've meditated on these things,
    I'll head contently back home
and drink my coffee sitting on the Southern ladder,
across from vegetables the dogs tore asunder in the night.

(1960)

Preámbulo a un nocturno

Caen las páginas,
los brazos ya no quieren soportar las palabras.
La luz cae igualmente de mis dedos,
y el cuarto se estremece, de pronto,
entre las sombras.

Y noto el vaho muriente de las últimas lámparas
llegar a mi ventana,
como luz de un entierro lejano por la noche,
como humo de tabaco
de hombres sin tierra alguna cavilando en la niebla.

Se derraman entonces los años y las noches —
los días perdidos en el pueblo oscuro —,
cuando la lluvia hablaba de un muchacho sin viajes
y el olvido goteaba largamente su hastío.

(California, 1958)

Preamble to a Nocturne

Pages fall,
the arms are already tired of holding words.
Light also falls from my fingers,
and the room shudders, suddenly,
amidst shadows.

I notice the last lamps whose dying vapor
reaches my window,
like light from a burial, distant and nocturnal,
like tobacco smoke
from landless men who ponder the mist.

That's when they spill, years and nights—
the days lost in this dark town—,
when the rain spoke of an unworldly boy
and oblivion lengthily dripped its tedium.

(California, 1958)

Luego

Cuando acabes mi vino
búscame en tus cadencias,
no hallarás mi alegría en ninguna de ellas,
y dirás sin pensar: . . .

Cuando acabes tu farsa
torna el rostro a mi ausencia;
recréate y prepara el vino del siguiente;
no acabará tu nombre donde empieza mi historia,
porque llevas mil rutas atadas a la frente.

Pero nada es olvido mientras existan huellas;
aunque siembres espinas sobre mi último sueño
el recuerdo primero tumbará tus anhelos,
y cuando vuelva el tiempo a pronunciar tu sombra
ya contarán tus culpas por todos los caminos.

(1958)

Later

When you finish my wine
seek me in your cadences,
you won't find my joy in a single one,
and you'll thoughtlessly say:...

When you finish your farse
turn to face my absence;
entertain yourself, prepare wine for the next guest;
your name won't end where my story begins,
because you've tied a thousand routes to your brow.

But nothing is forgotten as long as there are tracks;
even if you grow thorns on my last dream
first, memory will knock down your desires,
and when time by and by pronounces your shadow
they'll tell tales of your wrongs on all the roads.

(1958)

La carne perdurable

Anda la noche abierta festejando abandonos;
ayer es hoy con su dolor desnudo
y tú vas al verano.

Si no te hubiese amado tras la fiesta
tal vez tu nombre fuese armonioso y fácil;
tal vez la lluvia,
mientras golpea las sienes
y tus manos son largas y bruscas y angustiosas,
no sonaría en las calles como un sordo con ruidos,
como un bolsillo roto,
como si fuésemos monedas en trapos y pañuelos.

Me evoco por tu espesa topografía de lluvias
y me asalta tu piel levantando tus lomas,
pródiga de aguaceros y palabras mojadas.

Cuando somos de agua volvemos y volvemos.

Por eso hay noches turbias y de calles angostas
que persiguen tu aliento y van a los hoteles
y allí agotan botellas llenas de algo perdido.

Así voy fabricando tu olvido oscuramente.
Aunque duele esta fiebre que sube a mi aposento
y recuesta su inútil deseo en la ventana.

(1958)

The Lasting Flesh

Night stays open to celebrate desertions;
yesterday is today with naked pain
and you head toward summer.

If I hadn't loved you after the party was over,
perhaps your name would be simple, harmonious;
perhaps the rain,
as it beats our temples
and your hands are long and brusque and stressful,
wouldn't be loud in the streets like a deaf man's noise,
like a ripped pocket,
as if we were coins wrapped in rags and scarves.

I'm evoked by your dense topography of rains
and your skin assaults me lifting your hills,
prodigious with downpours and wet words.

When we are of water we turn and return.

Which is why there are turbulent nights, with broad streets
that chase your breath and head to hotels,
where they empty bottles full of something lost.

That is how I darkly manufacture you forgotten.
Even if it hurts, this fever that comes up to my room
and presses its useless want against my window.

(1958)

Memoria fiel

Del mar arriban ciertos días a la tierra
y hay pájaros que piensan en el sur.

Posible es que mi corazón arda alegremente
al encontrarse con aquella tarde en Mazatlán,
cuando extinguimos aguardientemente
las últimas fogatas del verano.

Todavía la recuerdo bajo aquel jachalí
y el río sonando abajo.

(Había muchos senderos en los cañaverales
y la yerba era alta y cosquillosa.)

Mas también llegan días con el amar a cuestas:
el papiro doliente, aquel instante de la guerra,
y fechas arrugándose en los huéspedes.

(Aún su recuerdo es ancho para mi corazón.)

No olvido las negras palomas en Nueva York
y la tal noche que por diez centavos subí a ver las estrellas.

Pero hay mejores ratos,
mejores aún que la alegría de la nieve en Reno,
que las naranjas que giran todo el año en Frisco.

Día tras día las cáscaras que navegan el tiempo
traen alguna deuda, alguna pena,
algún sudor extraño que hace pensar en viajes.

(1961)

Faithful Memory

From the sea certain days disembark on land
and there are birds that daydream of the south.

My heart might happily burn
when running into that afternoon in Mazatlán,
when we aguardientely extinguished
the last bonfires of summer.

I still see her standing under that jachalí
as the river sang below.

(There were many paths through the cane fields
and the grass was tall and ticklish.)

Plus some days arrive with steep love:
the aching papyrus, that moment during the war,
and dates wrinkling up within their hosts.

(Even these memories are too broad for my heart.)

I don't forget the black pigeons of New York
and that night when, for a dime, I climbed up to see the stars.

But there are better times,
even better than the joy of Reno's snow,
than the oranges in Frisco that spin year-round.

Day after day the peels that sail through time
deliver some debt, some sorrow,
some strange sweat, a souvenir of these travels.

(1961)

Vestigios de pólvora

En la noche rabiosa,
después de aquel incendio y lamento,
quedamos muchos muertos y callados
en la agrietada luna de Korea.

(Charcos rojos mojaron el verano.)

Luego nos fuimos remendando
y otra vez
aprendimos a cantar canciones bajando otras montañas.

Mas,
si a cada día expiado
mi silencio es más hondo, más seguro,
aún escucho cierto ruido a fragmentos,
cual mensaje de hierro
con anotaciones de pólvora y tibio olor a sangre.

Así a veces me voy: taciturno en la noche;
débil en mi tarea de soldado ya viejo
que recuerda la guerra.

Gunpowder Vestiges

In the furious night,
after all that fire and lament,
many of us were left dead and silent
in the cracked Korean moon.

(Red puddles soaked summer.)

Later we started patching these selves
and learned once more
to sing songs descending other mountains.

But,
if with each atoned day
my silence is deeper, more secure,
I still hear something akin to fragments,
like an iron message
with gunpowder notes and a warm trace of blood.

Sometimes I wander like that: taciturn at night;
weak in my old soldier's mission,
remembering war.

III

LA FRENTE INCLINADA

III

THE BOWED BROW

Breve elegía al hermano caído

Te vi caer,
roto,
el cráneo despidiendo silbidos,
brazos y manos
como ramas desesperadas
y volviste agrietado a la tierra.

En mi recuerdo
habitas este duro pensamiento:
Sobre las rocas,
cabalgando el gatillo enemigo,
en la puerta del rifle,
y de momento,
roto,
partido en dos como una vara seca,
con ruido de astillas gritando.

Sabrá Dios
como la tierra te acogió;
qué ritmos tocará la lluvia
en la marimba hueca de tus huesos.

Yo, sin embargo,
sigo con mi tristeza de hombre alegre,
a veces exclamando:
Si tu recuerdo fuese una mano extendida.

Y otras veces
poniendo los pies en la tierra,
con deseos
de encontrarte otra vez,
Hermano mío.

Brief Elegy to a Fallen Brother

I saw you fall,
broken,
skull sparking hisses,
arms and hands
like desperate branches,
and, cracked, you fell back to the earth.

In my memory
you inhabit this hard thought:
over the rocks,
riding the enemy trigger,
at the rifle's door,
and suddenly,
broken
in two like a dry rod,
your kindling screaming.

God knows
how the soil received you;
what rhythms the rain beat
on the hollow marimba of your bones.

I, on the other hand,
keep up my happy man's grief,
sometimes exclaiming:
If only your memory were an offered hand.

And other times
I am coming back down to earth;
I am wanting
to find you again,
my Brother.

Señalamiento

A Pedro Juan Brull

Quería decirte, Pedro Juan,
en el bronco lenguaje que viajo desde Humatas,
tus colinas verbales, tus poemas
de viento huracanado y luz inquieta.

Hace tardes éramos amigos;
bien sea,
había ya galopado tu recinto de imágenes
y en él te sorprendí con "los puntos en alto"
denunciando este inútil otoño del coraje.

Pensé acaso en tu vida como una gran cosecha:
tus siembras colectivas eran como esperanzas de graneros que estallan.

Y tú allí repartiendo tus frutos solidarios,
con algo de Walt Whitman en tu voz formidable,
"como el mar en la tierra", amigo Juan.

Ahora voy a tu orilla,
a tu clara frontera de palabras en lucha
por destruir las sombras amargas del ultraje.

Sigue, pues, dilatando tu ancha voz redentora,
crecida ya en la furia de un viejo desencanto;
como luz recorriendo los antiguos sembrados,
buscando las semillas pujantes de la aurora.

Ya nunca será tarde, Pedro Juan;
aún cuando la ignorancia nos haya sobornado
tu comarca de versos, tu región de metáforas
seguirán entonando tus zafras proletarias.

(continued)

Pointing Out

For Pedro Juan Brull

I wanted to tell you, Pedro Juan,
using coarse words that I ride from Humatas,
across your verbal slopes, your poems
of hurricaned wind and impatient light.

It's been many afternoons since we were friends;
rightfully so,
I had already galloped across your range of images
and there I surprised you with "raised points"
denouncing this useless autumn of rage.

I thought perhaps your life was a great harvest:
your collective sowings were like hopes for granaries exploding.

And there you were sharing your solidary fruits,
with some Walt Whitman in your formidable voice,
like "the sea pushes upon the land," my friend Juan.

Now I go to your shore,
to your clear frontier of words battling
to destroy insult's bitter shadows.

Continue, go ahead, dilating your broad redemptive voice,
already risen in the fury of an old disenchantment;
like light roaming ancient fields,
searching for dawn's thriving seeds.

It will never be too late, Pedro Juan;
even when ignorance has bribed
your verse district, your metaphor region
will still hum proletariat harvests.

(continued)

Recibe, pues, este señalamiento de Hermanos
que me lleva hacia tu red de versos,
hacia la "nasa", como dices tú.

Así he de continuar reclamando tus huellas,
tus corajes,
tu lengua levantada contra falsa praderas,
y me escuchas gritar alguna vez:
"Amarra tus leones, Pedro Juan,
que estoy entre tus vegas con mis armas!"

(1963)

Receive, this pointing by Brothers
that drives me to your net full of verses,
all the way to "nasa," as you like to say.

That's how I'll keep claiming your imprints,
your rages,
your language raised against false prairies,
and sometimes you'll hear me yell,
"Tie up your lions, Pedro Juan,
for I am roaming your meadows, well-armed!"

(1963)

Carmen Dolores

¡Carmen Dolores!
y parece que el viento va cargado de ajíes.

¡Ay, Carmen Dolores!
con tu cuerpo de azúcar lleno de hormigas bravas.
Tú eras la reina exacta del trópico en mis venas.

¿Acaso andarás hoy doblando mariposas;
o te empeñas en ser correo de ardientes plenas
navegando en licores?

Dulce Carmen Dolores,
que divertías mi risa con tu picante garbo
y tus melosos gestos espesos de ciclones.

Ven, cuéntame tus zafras de borrachas espigas —
háblame sobre el cielo grave y lento de Añasco.

¿Es El Recreo la calle que te llevó a tu selva,
o sólo una mentira empapada de rones?

Noble Carmen Dolores,
ven échame en la sangre la voz de tus tambores.

        *   *   *

Se destruyen los días con su gente menuda
y sólo tú me dueles, fina Carmen Dolores.

Sola sobre la historia inútil de tu pueblo
que te recuerda siempre
como una avispa negra cubierta de albayaldes.

(1958)

Carmen Dolores

Carmen Dolores!
and it seems the wind is loaded with ajíes.

Oh, Carmen Dolores!
with your sugar body full of red ants.
You were the exact queen of the tropics in my veins.

So, are you folding butterflies today;
or do you insist on being the messenger for fiery plenas
sailing the liqueurs?

Sweet Carmen Dolores,
who entertained my laughter with your stinging wit
and your syrupy gestures thick with cyclones.

Come, tell me your harvests full of drunken spikes—
speak to me of Añasco's grim and heavy sky.

Is El Recreo the street that led you to your jungle,
or only a lie soaked in rums?

Noble Carmen Dolores,
come pour your drums' voice into my blood.

*   *   *

Days are devastated with their petty people
and only you make me ache, rare Carmen Dolores.

You stand alone above your town's useless history,
that remembers you always
as a black wasp covered in electric ants and white lead.

(1958)

Elegía al Che Guevara

Su cadáver estaba lleno de mundo.
César Vallejo

Leyendo terremotos y tornados,
gritos amordazados y rojos aluviones,
revuelco semanarios, suplementos:
"Match". "La septieme mort de 'Che' Guevara",
y sus dos rostros barbudos de jornadas.

Nuestro ciego almanaque devora hojas,
y el pergamino espeso de la selva
reclama su asteriscada sangre
brillando bajo la Cruz del Sur;
mientras los cóndores,
pensándolo en la sierra
agitan el contenido aire
para ayudarle con su prieta asma.

Recoged el aliento,
contenedlo,
para cimbrar ese dolor andino
y luego dispararlo contra el mundo,
hacia la sangre desarmada,
este duro perfil americano.

¡Ah, Bolivia!
no hay lluvias suficientes en tus montes
para borrar
tanta sangre guerrera guevarina,
tanto norte en las sombras:
Porque vaya que murió despierto,
y tan alerta,
que su mirada trepa hasta los astros
y ellas bajan:
a iluminar su pecho, sus muñones,
sus tristes ojos suramericanos.

(continued)

Elegy for Che Guevara

His corpse was full of world.
César Vallejo

Reading earthquakes and tornados,
muzzled screams and red floods,
I rummaged through weekly papers, supplements:
"Match." "La septieme mort de 'Che' Guevara,"
and its two faces bearded with workdays.

Our blind almanac devours leaves,
and the jungle's thick parchment
demands his asterisked blood
shining under the Cruz del Sur;
while the condors,
thinking he is in the mountains
beat the contained air
to help with his constricted asthma.

Catch your breath,
contain it,
to shore that Andean pain
and then shoot it against the world,
toward unarmed blood,
this tough american profile.

Oh, Bolivia!
there is not enough rain in your mountains
to erase
so much Guevarean warrior blood,
so much North in the shadows:
Because boy did he die awake,
and so alert
that his gaze climbs to the stars
and they come down:
to illuminate his chest, his stumps,
his sad South American eyes.

(continued)

II

Mientras acá nosotros
hablamos del alucinado;
nos sorbemos su nombre copa a copa —
empinando ligeramente el codo,
bebiéndonos alegremente el tiempo —
rezando por los poros,
robándonos el pan de cada día,
y en este suelo inhóspito a los héroes
guardamos el insomnio
en una libretita recamada.

III

Y entretanto,
¿Adónde va la sangre de Guevara;
qué oscura planta,
qué árbol de vigilia la recibe y convierte?
¿Qué ha sido de sus huesos;
qué clandestina tierra los devora?

¿Dónde van sus cenizas;
qué viento, qué lluvia descentrada
las dispersa y disuelve?

Pero no demandemos las respuestas —
hijas feroces del anonimato —;
aunque sabemos que la tierra crece,
y cada arteria levanta en su remonte
un poco de la altura de su frente.

El árbol que la luna desentierra
esconde un largo viento entre sus ramas.
La mansa lluvia que en abril desciende
viajará luego en implacables aguas.

(continued)

II

While over here
we speak of the wild visionary;
we sip his name glass to glass—
slightly raising the elbow,
happily drinking up time—
praying through the pores,
stealing our daily bread,
and on this soil inhospitable to heroes,
we put away insomnia
in a small embroidered notebook.

III

And meanwhile,
where does Guevara's blood go;
what dark plant,
which vigil tree receives and converts it?
What has become of his bones;
what clandestine land devours them?

Where do his ashes go;
what wind, what unfocused rain
scatters and dissolves them?

But let us not demand answers—
fierce daughters of anonymity—;
even if we know the earth grows,
and each artery carries up in its lift
some of his forehead's height.

The tree the moon unearths
hides a long wind in its branches.
The gentle rain descending in April
will travel later across implacable waters.
(continued)

IV

¿Y nosotros?

No es mencionar la muerte:
es estar junto al muro y frente a ella,
en su lícita o fiera campanada.

Una sombra cavila tras la tapia,
el sol en este lado canta.

Muchos héroes del verso te han nombrado
con una aguda muerte entre sus manos;
(aunque la muerte sea canción perenne
que llevamos prendida en el regazo.)

No es el coraje frágil,
sino la densa y laboriosa fuerza
la que da al hombre su fijeza clara.

Los que al hombre por el hombre aman
caen bajo la metralla…

V

¿Por dónde vas, Amor?
¿Por dónde vas, Rencor?
¿Por dónde vas, Piedad, Dolor, Canción…?
¿Por dónde vas?

(continued)

IV

And what about us?

It's not the mention of death:
it's being up in front and against the wall,
in its licit or fierce chime.

A shadow ponders behind the wall,
the sun on this side sings.

Many verse heroes have named you
with a sharp death in their hands;
(even if death is a perennial song
we carry aflame in our laps.)

Courage is not fragile,
but rather the dense and laborious force
that gives man his clear fixity.

Those who love man for man's sake
fall under a hail of gunfire...

V

How far are you, love?
How far are you, Rancor?
How far are you, Mercy, Pain, Song...?
How far are you?

(continued)

Porque para llegar hasta tu nombre
tengo que apercibir mi corazón;
en la álgida noche
dejarlo junto al fuego,
frente a las huellas del jaguar;
cercado de altos gritos,
difícil el latido,
vigilante la piel...

Para regocijarme con tu afecto
tengo que dispensar mi único predio —
entregárselo al hombre —
al que redobla su machete,
al que apremia los bueyes,
al que remueva la semilla,
dándole duro al costado de la tierra.

Al que agobia su espalda,
y su frente es arrugado yunque
por martillos de sol, de sal y otoños.

Y enfrentarme
al gran juntacabezas,
al que bien las encoge,
al que bien las ajusta,
al que bien las vendimia,
al que bien las refriega, adorna y dora,
y luego las entierra...
Democráticamente.

(continued)

Because to reach your name
I have to warn my heart;
in the sweltering night
leave it by the fire,
in front of jaguar tracks;
surrounded by high-pitched calls,
the heartbeat struggles,
the skin is vigilant...

To rejoice in your affection
I have to release my only possession—
hand it over to the man—
who machete-rolls,
who drives the oxen,
who removes the seed,
forcefully striking the earth's side.

Who burdens his back,
whose forehead is an anvil wrinkled
by hammers of sun, salt, and autumns.

And I have to face
the great puzzle,
the one who compresses them well,
who adjusts them well,
who harvests them well,
who scrubs, adorns, and gilds them well,
and later buries them...
Democratically.

(continued)

Y para llegar a tu dolor
tengo que ir por las lluvias,
por los desfiladeros,
por la apretada selva,
entre lianas, venenos, mucha asma—
entre letales ritmos
cansado hasta la muerte,
pero alerta:
puntal en el decreto de fatiga
de quien ofrenda al hombre todavía
su iluminado corazón.

VI

¿Pero levantaré mi inútil signo
y viajaré la estela de tu sangre?
Tan fácil es decir:
"Esta es la tierra,
tú eres el hombre":
dilapidando el tiempo de los dioses,
quebrada la mañana en los costados.

(Desorbitado en el poema,
alucinado por la luz,
ebrio de círculos—
fatuo pájaro náufrago
girando en su canción.)

VII

Quién pudiera
desenterrar al hombre que en mí habita:
aunque fuese acogerme
para guijarro de su honda,
para sus tensas cuerdas,
o para el arco de su corazón.

(continued)

And to reach your pain
I have to cross the rains,
the gorges,
the crowded jungle,
among lianas, poisons, so much asthma—
among lethal rhythms
tired to death,
but alert:
punctual in decreeing the collapse
of he who still offers man
his enlightened heart.

VI

But will I raise my useless sign
and will I travel your blood's wake?
It's so easy to say:
"This is earth,
you are man":
squandering the gods' time,
morning shattered in our sides.

(Wild-eyed in the poem,
dazzled by the light,
drunk on circles—
fatuous shipwrecked bird
spinning in its song.)

VII

Who then could
dig up the man who lives in me:
even if only to accept
a pebble for his sling,
for its taut strings,
or for your heart's bow.

(continued)

Porque la piedra —
deleznable o común —,
si lanzada
con fuerza y con amor,
puede romper el aire,
sostenerse un instante en el vientre del tiempo
y encontrar de repente su destino
de arma de cazador.

¿Quién me lanza?
¿Quién es el justo hondero?
¿Por qué caminos andará Guevara?

VIII

Miro a mis niños
y tiento mi coraza;
Miro a mis libros,
Miro a las paredes que sostienen los libros
(o que los libros siempre han sostenido.)

Miro a la mujer,
su traje bien cansado,
su lugar en la mesa,
y un mantel bordado por sus manos
traduce mi sentencia.

Miro a los muebles
las lámparas, los cuadros,
el horror de la alfombra…

Yo que pensé que el hombre era una arteria
de viva luz,
sin límites o nudos.

(continued)

Because the stone—
despicable or common—,
if launched
with strength and with love,
can break the air
suspended for a moment in the belly of time
and can suddenly discover its destiny
as the hunter's weapon.

Who will throw me?
Who is the just slinger?
What roads might Guevara be roaming?

VIII

I look at my children
and my hand flies to my breastplate;
I look at my books
I look at the walls that hold the books
(or that books have always held.)

I look at the woman,
her exhausted dress,
her place at the table,
and a tablecloth her hands embroidered
translates my sentence.

I look at the furniture
lamps, paintings,
that horror, the carpet ...

I who thought that man was an artery
of vibrant light,
lacking boundaries or knots.

(continued)

Y aquí me acecho:
Anclado, anestesiado,
el soporífero orden familiar;
fraguando un día sin alas,
sembrando monederos viciosos
en el corazón de la mañana.

IX

No soy el Héroe,
tampoco soy el Hombre;
soy tan sólo huevo resonando.

Quedan muy pocos héroes en la tierra.

Pero estarán aquí,
ahora y entonces,
y siempre y para siempre,
porque tan sólo basta
que un hombre en pie arda en su coraje
y haga reclamar la Tierra.

Mientras tanto,
no habrá muerto Guevara para el hombre
ni el hombre abandonado al Che Guevara.

And here I lie in wait:
Anchored, anesthetized,
by soporific family order;
forging a wingless day,
planting vicious purses
in the heart of morning.

IX

I'm not the Hero
neither am I Man;
I am just a resonating egg.

There are very few heroes left on earth.

But they will be here,
now and then,
and always and forever,
because we just need
one man to stand up and burn in his rage
and make the Earth demand.

In the meantime,
Guevara will not be dead to man
nor will man have abandoned Che Guevara.

IV

SERAFIN ARMADO

IV

ARMED SERAPH

Canción de varias palabras

Así mi vida es una fuga y todo lo pierdo
y todo es del olvido, o del otro.

Jorge Luis Borges (Borges y yo)

Surge tu voz como las hojas, Borges.
Borges es voz sonando entre las hojas.
Tu voz anda por las hojas, Borges.
Borges es voz multiplicada en hojas.

Borges, tu voz se pierde a veces entre hojas.
Ya caen las hojas sobre la voz de Borges.
Borges, tú sabes que tu voz de hojas,
hojas será para otras voces, Borges.

(1967)

Song with Several Words

Thus, my life is an escape and I lose it all
and all is memory lost, or belongs to someone else.

Jorge Luis Borges (Borges and I)

Your voice, it rises like the leaves, Borges.
Borges is voice that sings among the leaves.
Your voice roams over the leaves, Borges.
Borges is voice when multiplied as leaves.

Borges, your voice sometimes gets lost in the leaves.
Leaves are now falling over the voice of Borges.
Borges, you know that your voice of leaves,
is now leaves for other voices, Borges.

(1967)

Fiesta a Dylan

¡Para que tu muerte sí tenga señorío!

Mañana, Dylan Thomas, será tu noche
y vamos a invitar a las brujas de Cader Peak
a que bailen tu fiesta.

Invocaremos a Li-Po y al compañero Omar:
(Y llenaremos los cuartos de humo
y algún olor a ron que nunca hayas probado.)
"Antaño,
antes del comienzo de la Eternidad,
sabía Alá
que habríamos de beber,
Estaba escrito..."

Por eso invitaremos a los seres extraños que tanto amabas,
a la bebida ardiente
y a las esposas de tus amigos.

(Nadie habrá de inquirir tu lúbrica belleza,
ni sabotear su duro contenido.)
Siento Dylan el deseo de traerte felicidad.
"[Seremos] los señores del mundo.
Todo el vino,
tanto el viejo como el nuevo,
lo hemos comprado."

"...y así, juntos bebiendo, el. pesar de mil años,
al fin, lograremos que huya."
"[Porque] un vaso de vino iguala vida y muerte
y mil cosas que cuesta demostrar..."

Tu piel sea con nosotros, Samuel Bennett,
mientras empollan los tigres sus criaturas.

(1963)

A Party for Dylan

So that your death may finally have its dominion!

Tomorrow, Dylan Thomas, will be your night
and we'll invite the witches of Cader Peak
to dance at your party.

We'll invoke Li-Po and compañero Omar:
(And we'll fill the rooms with smoke
and a slight whiff of a rum you've never tried.)
"Yesteryear,
before Eternity began,
Allah knew
we'd be drinking,
It was written..."

That's why we'll invite the strange beings you so loved,
the fiery drink,
and your friends' wives.

(No one will inquire as to your lubricious beauty,
nor sabotage its hard contents.)
I feel Dylan the desire to bring you joy.
"[Let us] lord over the world.
We buy new wine and old,
our cups to fill."

"Hand them to the boy to exchange for good wine,
And we'll drown away the woes of ten thousand generations!"
"But drinking makes us one with life and death,
 the myriad things we can barely fathom..."

Your skin be with us, Samuel Bennett,
while tigers hatch their cubs.

(1963)

A Virginia

Ya era tiempo, Virginia,
de rescatarle al verbo su estatura.

Hemos articulado tantos signos
que tal vez olvidamos el lenguaje inicial.

Pero has de recordar que fui tu rastreador—
peregrino de yerro y sinrazón—
fatigando las huellas de tu encuentro.

Tú apocabas callada mi distancia
y una mañana te sorprendí la espera,
y pensaste que hay ratos en la vida
dignos de despejar los brazos y entregarse.

Fuiste una mirada de paisaje encendido,
y mientras contemplaba
enriscada de luz tu cabellera,
un deseo vivísimo de amarte
desde mi corazón voló en abrazo.

Entonces conociste
toda la antigüedad de mis deseos.

Yo te invitaba
a convivir conmigo la tristeza
de veinticinco años de caminos.

Era como gritándote:
Levanta mi recuerdo y dale arcilla,
moldéalo en la fragua de tu aliento,
que el tiempo que nos mira con encono
tenga que declarar:
si un hombre se conmueve
la tierra se levanta, reverdece,
y anuncia una vendimia.   *(continued)*

144

For Virginia

It was about time, Virginia,
to rescue and return the verb's stature.

We articulated so many signs
that perhaps we forgot our first language.

But I ask that you remember I was your tracker—
pilgrim of madness in my iron erring—
wearing down the footprints of your encounter.

You silently whittled my distance
and one morning I surprised your wait,
and you thought how there are times in life
worth clearing out arms for a surrender.

You were fields aflame in a gaze
and while I contemplated
your hair curled and craggy with light,
a vividly alive desire to love you
flew from my heart in an embrace.

Then you knew
all the antiquity of my desires.

I invited you
to live together in the shared sadness
of twenty-five well-traveled years.

It was like I screamed:
Lift my memory and give it clay,
mold it in your forging breath,
so that time, acrimoniously staring,
is forced to declare:
if a man is moved deeply,
the earth will rise, will green
announcing a harvest. *(continued)*

Recibiste de pronto mi nostalgia:
yo había mirado más cielos que tú lámparas
y viajado más ríos que tú lágrimas,
y acaso ni guardaba
una pequeña devoción entre las manos.

Porque he vivido como un caracol,
como una concha en viaje y sin destino
fabricando estrellas bajas,
resbalosas,
para poder errar por este mundo.

Y esa zozobra varó en tu corazón;
le dijo quedamente:
Transitemos unidos esta noche;
detrás de cada puerta vive un duende,
giran hacia las sombras los ojos que recuerdan,
pero hay luches moviéndose a lo lejos.

Y así hemos trabajado esta jornada
en que se inician
los nuevos cazadores de vida,
nuestras albas asignaturas de amor.

Que se diga, Virginia:
no ha malogrado el tiempo ni tu voz ni tu aliento,
ni las profundas huellas de tus manos.

(1969)

You soon received my nostalgia:
I'd seen more skies than you'd seen lamps
and traveled more rivers than you did tears,
and failed to keep
a small devotion in my hands.

Because I've lived as a seashell,
a conch traveling with no destination,
fabricating low-hanging,
slippery stars,
so I may blunder across this world.

And this capsizing beached on your heart;
spoke to it in stillness:
Let us travel together tonight;
behind each door lives a duende,
remembering eyes turn to face their shadows,
but there are lights moving in the distance.

And thus we worked this shift
where we initiate
life's newest hunters,
our dawning love assignments.

Let it be known, Virginia:
neither your voice nor your breath have cursed time,
nor the deep imprints of your hands.

(1969)

Guatemala

A Hugo Cerezo Dardón

Te recuerdo en la piedra, Guatemala,
Antigua en la mirada se detiene;
pienso al Quetzal y su abatida ala
y tu pisada en signos se contiene.

Vuela el paisaje de la madrugada,
desde la selva hasta la armada cumbre;
Río Dulce invita a la madera anclada
a recorrer la ola y su relumbre.

Tu estatura en volcanes elevada
se ahoga en Atitlán y resplandece
entre paredes de maíz doradas.

Ya Tikal desde el aire me estremece:
pensar que bajo el limo está grabada
una garra de sangre que enmudece.

(1971)

Guatemala

For Hugo Cerezo Dardón

You were in stone, Guatemala,
Ancient, arrested in the gaze;
I think of Quetzal's broken wing,
and your footsteps in a sign maze.

The landscape of the dawn takes flight,
from the jungle to the armed peak;
Dulce River asks anchored wood
to ride the wave, its lightning streak.

Your height in volcanos risen;
it drowns in Atitlán and then shines
within gilded corn walls, glistens.

From above, Tikal disquiets;
I think how it's etched under lime:
a bloody claw that goes quiet.

(1971)

Punto en la rosa

A Carmelo Rodríguez Torres,
el hermano encontrado.

Llego en enero
¡Y estoy frente a Tikal—
cara al asombro!

Se han roto las palabras,
ruedan por las perfectas escaleras,
caen,
y la mirada hurga las paredes:
¡Se enardece!

¡La semilla!
aquí estuve,
anduve estos caminos;
esta selva
participa del memorioso círculo.

En este territorio del olvido
me cuidé del jaguar;
atavié me corteza
y honré a mi venerable Estrella de la Tarde.

Esta es la tierra que mis ojos vieron,
y que animó mi sangre.
Aquí habitó mi ira
y también mi ternura.

A los hombres de palo
insuflé mi agonía
y poblé de maíz
mis coyunturas.

(continued)

Point on the Rose

For Carmelo Rodríguez Torres,
a found brother.

I arrive in January
I'm in front of Tikal—
facing surprise!

The words have broken,
bouncing across the perfect stairs,
they descend,
and the gaze rummages the walls:
Inflamed!

The seed!
I've been here before,
I walked these paths;
this jungle
is part of the memorious circle.

On this territory of oblivion
I watched out for the jaguar;
I dressed my tree bark
and honored my venerable Evening Star.

This is the land my eyes took in,
that animated my blood.
Here lived my ire
and my tenderness as well.

With my agony,
I insufflated stick men
and populated my joints
with corn.

(continued)

Ahora regreso;
ciego frente a estos muros,
estas duras columnas,
este granito,
que inmovilizó el tiempo
y guarda una pisada en alto vilo,
una luna decrépita y ceñida.

Aquí,
vuelvo, regreso,
¡Oh Patria milenaria...!

Aquí he reconocido otra estación
¡mi tramontado viaje!

Aquí estoy,
aquí el milagro de un signo en el camino.

Now I return;
blindly facing these walls,
these hard columns,
this granite
which immobilized time,
with a footstep suspended on a highwire,
a decrepit and girdled moon.

Here, I come back, I return,
oh, millenary Patria!

Here I recognize another station and season,
my transmountainous journey!

Here I am,
here the miracle of a road sign.

Espejos

Reconocer

¿Cuándo somos de veras lo que somos?

Octavio Paz

Por la ruta que llevo va otro hombre
idéntico en fortuna y equipaje;
tal vez haya iniciado el mismo viaje,
y sólo nos distinguen por el nombre.

Tal vez a nadie este secreto asombre,
ni aún en su laberíntico andamiaje;
que ha ordenado la efigie de mi traje
a la ancha latitud de su pronombre.

Por los turbios meandros de ese espejo
tal vez giro hacia el fondo, él va remando,
permutando en las olas mi reflejo.
O tal vez él regresa y yo me alejo,
y yo por los caminos voy cantando
y en mi canción su tránsito festejo.

(1973)

Mirrors

To acknowledge

When do we truly become what we are?

Octavio Paz

Another man is on the path I walk,
both the same in fortune and in baggage;
it may be we venture down the passage,
where only names are made of different stock.

Could be this secret offers no one shock,
despite its labyrinthian package;
within, the effigy: my dinner jacket,
measured to fit his pronoun like a frock.

Crossing turbid meanders of mirror,
perhaps I face the back, he rows across,
rippling waves, my face, and then the steerer.
I, perhaps, float off, or he rows nearer,
or, on the road, I sing his joy and loss,
and, singing, rejoice his path is clearer.

(1973)

Las declinaciones

Juego mi vida, cambio mi vida
de todos modos la llevo perdida...

León de Greiff

Sólo nos queda un llanto que no llueve
y una cerrada llave a la ternura;
una canción vacía en que se apura
la voz que inútilmente se nos muere.

Nos queda un cielo oscuro que se mueve,
de untuosos peces y marea cansada;
un niño en cuya orífica mirada
la aurora ni se goza ni conmueve.

Nos queda un sueño de cemento ardido;
un serafín armado de pasquines,
una luz de neón dorando el filo.

Y si por agua y aire voy perdido,
sólo habrá de alentarme hacia mis fines
la inexorable llama del olvido.

(1963)

Declensions

I gamble with my life, change my life,
either way, I've lost...

León de Greiff

All that's left is grief that won't rain
and a locked key to tenderness;
an empty song whose hastiness
leads our dying voice in tired strain.

What's left are the clouds moving with chains
made of slick fish and tired tide;
and a boy's orificious eyes
find in the dawn no glee or gain.

Left is a dream of scorched cement,
a seraph armed with his leaflets,
and neon gilding knife's descent.

If air and water disorient,
I will find my way soon as I let
forgetting flame me forth unbent.

(1963)

Límites de la criatura

Pero los días son una red de triviales miserias
Jorge Luis Borges

Abrir el día
visitar sus costumbres
el diario resplandecer del eco
lo que ayer enunciamos
esto aquello lo mismo inalterable
mirar la antigua casa
la borrada huella
el pájaro sin ruidos
torvo la luz fatiga y seca el agua
no se mueve la rueda
y agostado el perfume
se pudre en el jardín abandonado
el ojo ya no encuentra
la luz cerrada de la puerta
ni asiste a su ventana acarcelada
no vamos por la sangre
débiles atrapados
en el embudo de este corazón
no se amanece ni se piensa el día

ir a la noche
mirar sus caries sus oscuras armas
su arrepentida luz
la estrella rota junto a la cloaca
el viento contenido
tirado recostado inexpresivo
oh días horas minutos
bien ardidos
de botellaenbotella y tiempo muerto
estrujado vivir de esta criatura
de este ilustreinútildesgraciado.

diciembre del 72

Creature Limits

But the days are a network of trivial miseries
Jorge Luis Borges

To start the day
visit its customs
the daily shine of its echo
what yesterday we declared
this that the same inalterable thing
to look at the ancient house
the blurry footprint
the noiseless bird
grim the light tires and dries the water
the wheel won't move
and the scorched perfume
rots in the abandoned garden
the eye no longer finds
the closed light of the door
nor assists its incarcerated window
we don't go for the blood
weaklings trapped
in this heart's funnel
we don't rise or think about the day

to go visit evening
look at its cavities its dark weapons
its remorseful light
the broken star near the sewer drain
the contained wind
lying on the ground inexpressive
oh days hours minutes
all ablaze
from bottletobottle and the dead harvest of time
the wrinkled living of this creature
of this illustrioususelessdesgraciado

December of '72

Elegía a mi lirofonía

[. . . aunque] El último verso nunca será cantado.

Vicente Huidobro

Añosa y destemplada compañera,
apenas te levanto hacia el clamor del día,
revisas tu cosecha,
y quebrantas los tallos de tu siega.

En la explanada hierven los metales,
viajan polígonos y torres;
mas no florece el pájaro en el aire,
ni el surco abre su triunfo.

Fatigada y remota se desplaza la tarde,
y no hay línea del cielo que nos llegue;
se viaje en noria rechinante,
y una sombra gradúa la mirada.

Pobre enfrentada mía:
clamas,
y revientas el vuelo de tu voz;
miras,
y asesinas tus mejores imágenes.

Eras la esperanzada:
en tus cuerdas templaba Humatas su corazón terroso,
alzando nuevamente la música del hombre
que por veredas y quebradas cantaba la fortuna de la tala
donde el maíz fraguaba su fiebre de pan tierno.

Y ahora, pobre y agonizante,
no importa la mañana con sus senos de luz levantando el espacio.

Ya no hay recodos que doblar
ni caballos que corran el poniente.

(continued)

Elegy to My Lirophony

[... although] The last verse will never be sung.

Vicente Huidobro

Aged and distempered compañera,
as soon as I wake you toward the clamor of day,
you check your crops,
and snap your harvest stalks.

Metals boil in the esplanade
with traveling polygons and towers;
still the bird doesn't bloom in the air,
and the furrow won't open its triumph.

Exhausted and remote the afternoon unfolds,
and the sky extends us no phone line;
we travel on a grinding Ferris wheel,
and a shadow graduates the gaze.

My poor confronted love:
you clamor,
and burst your voice's flight;
you glare,
and assassinate your best images.

You were the hopeful one:
Humatas tuned its muddy heart on your strings,
raising again the music of the man
who sang along paths and creeks the good fortune of felling
where corn forged its tender-bread fever.

And now, poor and dying,
morning doesn't matter with its luminous breasts lifting up space.

There are no more turns to bend
nor horses that race across the sunset.

(continued)

La cumbre es sombra detenida.
Abolida has de reconocer
que en tu predio no pulsa la templanza del fruto,
y dondequiera que asignas tu palabra
cae el ruiseñor.

Ahora, ¿qué nos resta?
Se pudre la semilla del verbo
y no encuentra raíz de donde asirse.
La metáfora humilde te abandona,
y se rodea de puños.

Derriba tu paisaje.

Que vengan los nuevos arcilleros
y de tu barro levanten otras músicas
que respondan al brío de la joven simiente.

Hora es de comprender
que todo lo que amaste va de paso,
y de tus mieses —
de tus días laboriosos —
sólo eres página harto terruñal
que va inútil y ajada hacia el fondo del libro.

The zenith is detained shadow.
Abolished you are to accept
that your estate doesn't pulse the fruit's temperance,
and wherever you assign your word
the nightingale falls.

Now, what remains?
Seed's verb rots
and finds no root to grasp.
The humble metaphor leaves you behind,
and surrounds itself with fists.

Your view topples.

May the new potters come
and raise other musics from your clay,
that will correspond to the verve of young seed.

It is time to understand:
all you loved is just passing through,
and of your crops—
of your laborious days—
you are but a very dusty and telluric page,
heading, useless and worn, toward the back of the book.

Notes

The Dark Town and a Gate to the Garden

The Town's Night p. 11

wasted   In translating "ebrio" as "wasted" and not "drunk" I open it to
more meanings, resonating with the general sense of exhaustion that
permeates the poem.

accustomed   "Acostumbrada" here can mean both "everyday" and
"accustomed." I am assuming word play in Rivera Avilés. Although it
might be argued that the alliteration of "acostumbrada" and "acera"
account for the word choice, it is an unusual word if meaning "everyday"
and likely an intentional choice over "cotidiana" or "diaria," both of
which would have had assonance with "acera."

my hands in their pockets   By using the articles "las" and "los" instead of
the possessive "mis," Rivera Avilés creates variation in repetition, but
also signals that the hands and pockets have a relationship not mediated
by the speaker.

The Dark Town p. 13

public cars   "Choferes públicos" refers to a public car service similar to
taxis, but more individuated and using old model cars.

jíbaros   An impoverished Puerto Rican peasant or field worker from a rural
area. Luis Muñoz Marín's populist rhetoric turned the jíbaro into an
archetypical figure. During the 1950s, this archetype presented the jíbaro
as humble, poor, somewhat naïve, and hardworking. Since Rivera Avilés
grew up in a rural town, his description of the life of a jíbaro and his
reclaimings of the term at times are verbally ironic and other times invert
the relationship between town and city by celebrating small town life as
preferable. See Juan Gelpí's *Literatura y parternalismo en Puerto Rico* for
more on the figure of the jíbaro in Puerto Rican literature.

the ship-filled shore / or the shores of ships   I have chosen to retain both
    meanings through repetition and the addition of a verse.

unattended   "Descuidadas" can translate as "careless," "unwatched,"
    or "uncared for/ unattended." I chose the latter use, since it most
    encompasses the others.

the poor eyes of the hanged poor   I choose to use "poor" as an adjective,
    though placed differently, and a noun, since the Spanish could be read both
    ways: as "hanged poor" and as "poor hanged".

to make and do nothing   The word "hago" in Spanish is much more
    generative in this context. "Hacer" is both to make and to "do" or "act."
    There is an intentional use of the idea of talking shit and doing nothing,
    but it is so tightly woven that I had to split "nada hago" into "make" and
    "do" and thus it lost a bit of the multilayered play in the last verse.

Storm   *p. 23*

a field of mirrors   Though it is not explicitly a field, "entre" here suggests the
    horses are running through and past the mirrors.

Muchacha en la ciudad   *p. 27*

Muchacha en la ciudad   The title in the Spanish version is in English, so I
    have inverted the relationship and put the title in Spanish in this version in
    order to recreate the contrast between the title and the body of the poem.

In my beard: winds and forests.   I have translated the alejandrino meter in
    Spanish to the decasyllable. Both are syllabic and not accentual-syllabic,
    which makes the English translation a bit strange. I feel that strangeness
    serves an echo of the other language's governing structure. I have tried to
    translate the syllabic variance in the second and fifth verses.

Story for Another History

Story for Another History   In Spanish "story" and "history" both translate as "historia," therefore, this title could also be translated as "Story for Another Story," "History for Another Story," or "History for Another History."

the same old forever   This can also be translated as "the same old shit" or "the same old things," but considering this is a poem that plays with temporality, the use of "siempre" doesn't feel coincidental, so I made the choice to play more overtly with the pun in my translation.

The Wait

my detached cat   This was a translation challenge since "flojo" has so many connotations. It can mean to be loose, to be loosened, to be limp, to be lame, or to be of bad quality. This last meaning is usually associated with shoddy craftsmanship and therefore laziness. The verse implies the cat is lazy but also limp on the ground. It's an unusual choice of words and links directly back to the metaphor of a "siesta" that gets tangled with both the cat's laziness and its limpness. I chose to play on the idea of a strap or rope that is attached, adding another possible reading: the cat as indifferent, the laziness as misread detachment.

country fields   "Casa de campo" means "country home," but the play on words would translate literally as "country and poem house."

Jíbara That Saw City

unsuccessfully searches for his goodbye   Here he is using a turn of the sexist and flirtatious expression, "Where is my goodbye?"

Then

cousin   Here some of the specificity of gender in the word "prima" is lost. I'm thinking of the popular Puerto Rican expression, "Los primos se exprimen," or "cousins squeeze each other." The poetic voice in this poem is a young picaresque boy, so a great deal of these verses have sexual or, at least, homosocial undertones.

1963

Friday, JUNE 28 *p. 47*

to the touch   "Al toque" can mean the first blast, the first strike, or the first
chime, but in this case, it also refers to the first touch of hands since
the word "toque" means "a touch." Since the "toques" are leading the
ripening, I concluded that the poet is also referring to a repeating chiming
or blasting, or a rhythm. I chose to combine "the touch of hands" and "to
the rhythm of the beat."

You Lose Nothing, Old Horse (Remedy Work)

A Sense of the Impossible *p. 53*

A Sense of the Impossible   Here "noción" is being used in a way that is
similar to "noción del tiempo," hence my translation.

I was shining shoes   For a time during his youth, Rivera Avilés worked
shining shoes.

Vocation *p. 59*

Patria   I chose not to translate patria. Neither "fatherland" nor "homeland"
capture the totality of its resonances. On the one hand, "fatherland"
has fascist and imperialist nationalist undertones that don't correspond
accurately to the anti-imperialist nationalism often found in colonies. On
the other hand, "homeland" is too vague and overlooks the patriarchal and
familial associations of "patria."

Thinking and Reviewing *p. 61*

left of zero   A play upon the expression "un cero a la izquierda" or a zero
placed to the left of a number. Here Rivera Avilés is punning on the "Left"
as a political term, a space where the "zeros" can organize a kind of hope,
and the poetic voice imagines that not even this "left" will leave a record.

Humatas

released   "Entregar" is to turn in, but is also used when referring to hostages who are released: "Se entregaron los rehenes."

Letter to the Sister

mesh   Rivera Avilés' use of "maya" (the phonetic spelling in Puerto Rican Spanish) instead of "malla" seems intentional and possibly a reference to the Mayan people, considering his time in Mexico.

Rainy Morning

common neighbor   There is a sexist double innuendo in "la vecina de todos," which references the popular expression, "la amante de todos," or "everyone's lover." The word "lover" is cleverly included in the verse, indicating the intentionality of this play on the expression. I chose to translate "de todos" as "shared" because in both cases there is a reference to promiscuity that is slippery, in which neighbor and lover are confused.

stings and burns   Again, "arder" can be to sting or to burn. The ambiguity of the word lies in the sliding scale of its intensity. The act of lovemaking can be a stinging or a burning, just as the neighbor can be a neighbor or a lover. Considering Rivera Avilés' rejection of Catholicism, it's safe to say that although there is a sexist, picaresque play on the neighbor's promiscuity, the notion of sinful, burning flesh is also defiantly embraced in a truly contradictory and Catholic fashion.

to be lazy / and have a woman in the kitchen   The "laziness" here is both the refusal to work and the refusal to examine set gender dynamics, such as the wife/woman's place in the kitchen. This is a common move for the poet. He often, in a disavowing manner, equals knowing complacency with a return to old ways.

Major Elegy to the Earth p. 79

It's best you turn around, you walk in circles   I slightly changed the line break here so the verses would flow in English.

a *duende*   Can either be an elf or sprite, or it can be (most likely given his interest in Lorca) an allusion to the notion of "duende" put forth in Federico García Lorca's essay, "Juego y teoría del duende."

your yard full of graves   "Campo de muertos" aludes to "camposanto" or "graveyard."

Mireya p. 99

Mireya does things   Although this would seem to translate literally into "Mireya has things that warm the days," it is actually an abbreviation of the common phrasing "Mireya tiene [cosas que hace] que hacen gratos los días" or "Mireya has things [she does] that warm the days."

evening's slip-and-falls   "Caída" means "fall" as well as "setting" when referring to the sun. The image is that of a sun that repeatedly slips and falls, thereby bathing the yard in red evening light.

singing bristled songs   I have tried to keep the ambiguity of the Spanish by leaving undetermined whether the flowers are singing Mireya's songs or whether she is singing as she plants the flowers.

East of Possible   "Lessueste" is an older usage of east, leading me to think
the title is alluding to *East of Eden*, the 1952 novel by John Steinbeck
(a copy of which he kept in his personal library), adapted into the film
version in 1955 by Elia Kazan. Given that Añasco is on the west coast
of Puerto Rico, and the tropicalism of Puerto Rico's construction in the
American imaginary as a "paradise," Rivera Avilés' choice to replace
"Eden" with "possible" suggests the possibility of a return to the Edenic,
while also suggesting the proximity of the present. We are just east of
what is possible. It is also in tune with his interest in a poetics of the
quotidian. Eden becomes a vegetable garden destroyed by dogs while the
poet wanders and muses on loss, yet, despite this loss of garden and love,
the poet returns "contently" to his home.

any drowsy bar   A play on the expression, "De cualquier malla sale un
ratón."

Pointing Out *p. 119*

Pointing Out   A "señalamiento" is a kind of critique (but less lengthy),
pointing out something that is wrong, that needs correcting.

range of images   There are many ways to translate "recinto," all of which
indicate a controlled and limited area or site. By using "range," I open up
that range of meanings. The images might be livestock grazing the range
and the speaker might be a cowboy or jíbaro riding across and observing.
But a "range of images" is also an limited array of images and can be read
as the speaker insulting his rival by suggesting his range is small enough
that he has already galloped across it; that he has a limited range.

raised points   A combination of points being raised and raised fists.

the sea pushes upon the land   See Walt Whitman, "Sea-Drift," *Leaves of
Grass: The First (1855) Edition*. New York: Penguin, 2005. Print.

Carmen Dolores

ajíes   Ajíes, or chili peppers (much like the electric ants I mention in the next footnote), are small and powerful.

electric ants and white lead   Albayalde translates as white lead, but "abayarde" is *Wasmannia auropunctata*, an electric ant or little fire ant. Since, in Puerto Rican Spanish, "l" and "r" are often interchanged, it makes me think Rivera Avilés wanted to evoke both the image of the black wasp covered in white paste and a black wasp being devoured by ants. White lead was used as the basis of most oil paints and in the decoration of houses, thus evoking both an older form of preservation and the decorative exterior (or superficial appearance) of the town people's private lives. Abayardes, or electric ants, are infamous in Puerto Rico for their painful bite, and are often used to exemplify a deceptive appearance, since they are small but powerful.

Elegy for Che Guevara

machete-rolls   As in drum-rolls with a machete.

Song with Several Words

leaves for other voices, Borges   In Spanish, the verses are variations of the endecasílabo. In English, I changed this to variations on the decasyllabic verse. Both are syllabic and irregular.

A Party for Dylan   Refers to the poet Dylan Thomas.

compañero Omar   Refers to the poet Omar Khayyam.

Yesteryear....It was written   It is unclear which translation Rivera Avilés
was using or if he was, in all probability, paraphrasing and rending in
Spanish Edward Fitzgerald's orientalist translation of Omar Khayyam's
Rubaiyat. London: (Mitre), 1947. The closest verses are, "Why, be this
Juice the growth of [Allah], who dare/ Blaspheme the twisted tendril as
a Snare?/ A Blessing, we should use it, should we not?/ And if a Curse —
why, then, Who set it there?"

   For more on Orientalism in the Latin America see Laura J. Torres
Rodríguez, "Diseños asiáticos: Orientalismo y modernidad en México"
(2012). *Dissertations available from ProQuest*. AAI3551784. *https://
repository.upenn.edu/dissertations/AAI3551784*

We buy new wine and old / our cups to fill   Also seems to be drawn from
Khayyam's *Rubaiyat*, perhaps Fitzgerald's translation, "We buy new wine
and old, our cups to fill,/And sell for two grains this world's good and ill;/
Know you where you will go to after death?/ Set wine before me, and go
where you will!"

Hand them to the boy....ten thousand generations   I have had to work with
various translations since Rivera Avilés seems to have drawn from various
translations in Spanish. See Li Bai, Witter Bynner, and Laozi. *The Chinese
Translations*. New York: Farrar, Straus, Giroux, pp. 120-121, 1978.

But drinking makes us....we can barely fathom   From the A. S. Kline
translation of Li-Po "Three Poems on Wine," *Like Water or Clouds: The
T'ang Dynasty and the Tao*. Luxembourg: Poetry in Translation, 2000.

Your skin be with us, Samuel Bennett, / while tigers hatch their cubs   A
perfect imitation of a quote from Dylan Thomas ends the poem. In the
original citation given in an interview Thomas expressed, "I wrote endless
imitations, though I never thought them to be imitations, but rather
wonderful original things, like eggs laid by tigers." See John Goodby.
Poetry of Dylan Thomas—under the Spelling Wall. Liverpool UP, 2014.

For Virginia p. 145

to rescue and return   By writing "rescatarle al verbo," the implication is that
the speaker and his accomplices will be rescuing the stature on behalf of
the verb, thus I've translated it as "rescue and return."

my iron erring   "Yerro" or "I err" is a homonym that when pronounced
sounds like "hierro" or "iron." I've tried to account for the echoes this
usage generates.

clearing out arms for a surrender   I've teased out a bit of a pun that isn't
quite there in the Spanish version but that I believe Rivera Avilés would
have enjoyed. The image of human arms as tall grass that needs to be cut
with a machete, thus opening a path in order for lovers to give themselves
fully to each other is stunning and generative. It leads me to think the
path being cut (as often was the case) might be heading toward a body
of water. However, there seems to be a subtle approach to the speaker's
own masculinity in this verse, since the speaker feels he must push clear
of both the influences of others and past loves in a forceful way so he can
reach Virginia. Given Rivera Avilés' recurrent use of bellicose terminology
and imagery, it felt right to collapse the meanings enclosed in the word
"arms" and play with the idea that to reach his loved one, the speaker
had to engage in a kind of war with the world and with himself, leading
to a form of defeat. This defeat is ultimately a win, leaving the reader
wondering if the aims of such a war actually benefit the speaker.

this capsizing beached on your heart   This translates most accurately as "that
capsizing," but, upon translating the poem into English, it became unclear
the poet was using "that" as a definite article and the repetition of "that"
later on also made it clunky. "This" makes it more intimate, but it still
works if we consider the usage within the larger context of the poem.

Guatemala p. 149

a bloody claw that goes quiet   In Spanish, Rivera Avilés uses slightly irregular
endecasílabo, which I changed to octosyllabic verse in English. Since
the rhyme in Spanish occurs in every verse, and in English I only rhymed
every other verse, I tried to compensate by making the octasyllabic verses
in English regular.

Point on the Rose

p. 151

Point on the Rose   Alluding to the compass rose, wind rose, or rose of the
winds.

this territory of oblivion   Allusion to Puerto Rico's colonial status as a U.S.
"territory."

Mirrors

p. 155

and, singing, rejoice his path is clearer   In Spanish, Rivera Avilés uses
irregular endacasílabo. I chose to use irregular decasyllabic verse in
English.

Creature Limits

p. 159

the dead harvest of time   There seem to be two allusions here. "Dead time"
might refer to the period of time when laborers, especially field laborers,
did not work the land, but in English it loses the association with death,
the idea that time no longer exists. I have combined both notions.

illustrioususelessdesgraciado   See my preface, "From Our Shared Disgrace:
Preface to Angel Dominguez' *Desgraciado*," *Desgraciado*, Nightboat
Books, 2022: "The word 'desgraciado' literally means he/she/they that
have fallen out of God's grace, to be a disgraced. Colloquially however, to
be a 'desgraciado' is to be despicable. *¡Eres un desgraciado!* was a terrible
insult for my grandmother's generation, it meant you were the worst of the
worst, and not even God could save you."

Elegy to My Lirophony

p. 161

compañera   "Compañera" is often mistranslated as "comrade," which would
be "camarada." "Compañera/o/e" is a term that can mean comrade,
romantic or business partner, or companion.

Following the Tracks in the Poetry of Sotero Rivera Avilés

Raquel Salas Rivera

T HE WORK OF SOTERO RIVERA AVILÉS IS KEY TO understanding how previously excluded Black and impoverished Puerto Ricans gained access to written literature through educational reforms, such as the G.I. Bill, as well as how this inclusion was ultimately conditional, forcing these writers to offer themselves up as, what Paul B. Preciado calls, experimental sites for "the new dynamics of advanced technocapitalism."[1] Born on April 28, 1933, in Añasco, Puerto Rico, Sotero Rivera Avilés was also my grandfather, a man who produced work that was extraordinary in its scope, most often writing in the lyrical style that was characteristic of the Guajana Group,[2] which included writers situated between the Generation of the Thirties[3] and the Generation of the Sixties.[4]

Unlike other writers of his generation, he also wrote about being a post-war veteran in a rural Puerto Rican town and the broken promises of Luis Muñoz Marín's populist modernization projects. He demystified the jíbaro archetype of the naïve, but good-hearted field laborer saved by mass migration to urban centers, such as San Juan and New York. He wrote openly about his disabilities, delved into the seldom described experiences of post-war reverse migration, and left a record of regionalisms from a world that no longer exists. His is some of the only poetry written about Humatas, his childhood barrio in Añasco, and he always insisted that the breadth of his work could never overshadow the importance of the life he led before acquiring a formal education. He has received little if any recognition outside

---

1. See Paul B. Preciado, *Testo Yonqui*, p. 27, Espa/Fórum, 2008.
2. Grupo Guajana
3. La generación del treinta
4. Generación del 60

of Puerto Rico. The first selection of his work and the first full-length translation of his poems, *The Rust of History: The Selected Poems of Sotero Rivera Avilés* is a recovery project that pays homage to the man without whom I would never have forged my love of poetry.

Sotero Rivera Avilés (1933–1994)

Like most Puerto Rican towns, Añasco, the town where Rivera Avilés grew up, was founded in 1733 and later oriented and organized around the production of sugar cane. My grandfather was one of many descendants of enslaved sugarcane workers. As a teenager, he worked after school in a bakery, making enough money to help care for his siblings. In an interview, his daughter and my mother, Yolanda Rivera-Castillo, described some of his upbringing. She explained that, "[His father] had arthritis, worked his whole life in a bakery and in agriculture. He had seventeen children with my grandmother, of which nine survived, the oldest of which was my father."[5]

When he was older, Rivera Avilés began working at a local bakery. Oftentimes he would work past ten at night and wake up at two in the morning to deliver bread all over town. He had to watch his ninth-grade and high school graduation processions through the bakery window. Despite these adverse circumstances, in high school, he was nicknamed "Potencia" or "Powerhouse" because he was able to earn good grades with little or no time to study. In addition to being an after-school laborer, he was also an intellectual worker, a paid strongman, and an amateur boxer. The wealthier students would pay him a quarter to do a variety of jobs including fighting their fights and writing their love letters.

In 1951, soon after graduating from high school, he enlisted in the US Marines. After a brief stay at Fort Buchanan, he was deployed to fight in the Korean War. Approximately two years later, in August,

---

5. In February, 2021, I interviewed my mother, Yolanda Rivera Castillo, about my father. The following biography is partially composed of interviews with her and with my grandmother, Virginia Castillo Beauchamp, that took place on the following dates: December 31, 2019; January 1, 2020; February 2, 2020; February 3, 2020; May 16, 2021; June 6, 2021; June 18, 2021; June 22, 2021; and July 19, 2021.

1953, at the age of twenty-one, he was wounded during his service.[6] As is detailed in the lawsuit filed after his death by his wife and my grandmother, Virginia Castillo Beauchamp, and by countless medical records, Rivera Avilés' wounds were extensive and included the mutilation of both his legs, the amputation of his left arm, "marked hyposthesis, hypoalgesia and anesthesia in areas of scarring below the knee, [...]permanent edema and loss of mass of his right leg," as well as "residual metal fragments form the explosion."[7]

During his post-war hospitalization in San Francisco, a local family came across his name on a list of wounded soldiers published in a local newspaper. They happened to share a last name. Basing their decision on this coincidental link, they took him into their home, and, with their support, Rivera Avilés began his undergraduate studies at San Mateo College, eventually obtaining an Associate degree in Arts after transferring to the University of Puerto Rico,

---

6. From the archival materials of Sotero Rivera Avilés, provided with the support of my family and, in particular, my grandmother and mother who sat down with me to look through the files. The report written at the U.S. Naval hospital in Pendleton, California, described the incident: "Patient was bystander in vicinity of explosion of missile (type?) in which three others were injured. Multiple lacerations as a result of missile explosion. Patient was at work cutting weeds. During 10-minute break they were sitting on a concrete tunnel. One of the marines was playing with a dud—one of many shells lying about on the ground—the dud slipped from his hand and hit the concrete. It exploded."

7. "On August, 1953, Mr. Rivera was nearly killed and grievously wounded, while on maneuvers, by the explosion of a missile. He was wounded and mutilated in his right leg, left leg, and following an amputation lost the left forearm and arm above the elbow joint. He also suffered a cardiac arrest while undergoing the operation for those wounds. He wore a prosthesis of the left upper extremity during the remainder of his life. He was also unable to perform any movement with the right foot as the ankle was fixed at 90°. He was forced to drive (had always use to) a specially fitted automobile to compensate for the infirmities listed above. His right inferior extremity had marked hyposthesis, hypoalgesia and anesthesia in areas of scarring below the knee. He suffered, in addition, permanent edema and loss of mass of his right leg. According to Mrs. Castillo he also had residual metal fragments from the explosion. Mr. Rivera was classified, and always remained with a 100% service-connected disability."

Mayagüez Campus. During his studies at San Mateo, he began writing his first poems, and self-publishing his first poetry books: *Nostalgia* (1957), *Abandonos* (1958), and *El Pueblo Obscuro y una puerta al jardín* (unknown date).

Before completing his undergraduate degree, he decided to travel through Mexico as an independent journalist and writer. Records of this period are sparse, but the call of Humatas was strong enough to bring him back to Puerto Rico in search of the "dark" and "small" town of his memory. What he found may not have aligned with those memories, but he did everything in his power to recreate the idyllic rural life he envisioned, including marrying a young woman from his hometown, my grandmother, on July 23, 1960, after which, they immediately began forming a family. Their oldest child, my mother, was born in 1961, followed by Sandra Rivera Castillo in 1963. Neftalí Rivera Castillo, my eldest uncle, was born in 1964, and Yamil Rivera Castillo was born in 1965. Both entered the world while the couple lived in Vega Baja. The youngest, Emir Rivera Castillo, was born in 1968.

In 1974, Rivera Avilés won the Premio Ventana for his poetry book, *Cuaderno de tierra y hombre*. A year later, after a brief period working for the International Life Insurance Company, he began teaching as an adjunct at the nearby Mayagüez Campus of the University of Puerto Rico and searching for a stretch of land where he could build a future home and live surrounded by fields and mountains in an environment similar to that of his childhood in Añasco.

Although, as previously mentioned, he is mostly associated with the Guajana Group, outside of literary journals, he shared few spaces with the group's most well-known writers, such as Vicente Rodríguez Nietzsche, Andrés Castro Ríos, José Manuel Torres Santiago, Marcos Rodríguez Frese, Wenceslao Serra Deliz, and Edgardo López Ferrer.[8] There existed another Guajana Group, based in cities such as Mayagüez, far from the cosmopolitanism of San Juan. There, his interlocutors were writers such as Carmelo Rodríguez Torres, a novelist from the neighboring island of Vieques, and Luis Cartañá,

---

8. See the Enciclopedia de Puerto Rico Entre for "Guajana: Grupo de poesía" (*https://enciclopediapr.org/content/guajana-grupo-de-poesia/*).

a Cuban-born poet who taught at the Mayagüez Campus alongside Rivera Avilés. With Rodríguez Torres and Jorge María Ruscalleda Bercedóniz, he founded the literary group Mester de poetas and the literary journal *homónima* (1967). As the poet Edgar Ramírez notes,[9] these three poets organized readings, mentored younger poets, and played a key role in literary circles on the West coast.

More than a decade after *Cuaderno de tierra y hombre*, in 1989, he self-published his last poetry book, *Nada pierdes, caballo viejo (Faena de remedios)*. Four years later, in 1993, he finished his first and only novel, *Con premeditación y alevosía: (Radiografía de un crimen)*. The following year, on October 27, 1994, the man described by military officers as "a well-developed, thin Puerto Rican male who is alert and cooperative," left us with the memory of a poet whose work was anything but complaisant. The government refused to adequately pay Virginia for the funeral and her living expenses, leading to a legal battle, which she eventually won. Instead of using the government check to pay for a traditional funeral, my grandmother decided to follow my grandfather's burial wishes. His body was cremated and his ashes were scattered over the mountains overlooking Humatas.

Early Works: *Nostalgia* (1957), *Abandonos* (1958), and *El Pueblo Obscuro y una puerta al jardín*

Rivera Avilés' poetics is in no way neatly predicated on dates or places. Although he successfully moved out of poverty, he paid with his participation in the war, the loss of an arm, and a life full of physical and psychic trauma. In his retellings, the Korean War meant the death of his younger self and the birth of a poet, but it also "water bellies"[10] where lost time could swell into nostalgia. Much of his poetry is composed of memories strung together as if he were trying to construct solidity itself. Rivera Avilés still lived in the diaspora when he wrote and published his first three poetry books and began exploring the relationship between trauma, memory, and the colonial

---

9. On June 23, 2021, I had the pleasure of interviewing Edgar Ramírez on his own work and his relationship with this group of poets for El proyecto de la literatura puertorriqueña/ The Puerto Rican Literature Project.

10. See "Elegía mayor a la tierra" and my translation "Major Elegy to the Earth."

legacy of writing. *Nostalgia* (1957), *Abandonos* (1958), and the unpublished typewritten manuscript *El Pueblo Obscuro y una puerta la jardín* (unknown date) contained many of the elements that would go into his 1974 collection, *Cuaderno de tierra y hombre* (1974). Both *Cuaderno* and *El Pueblo Obscuro*, for example, open with the same epigraph: two verses by Pablo Neruda.[11] *El Pueblo Obscuro* also contains an early version of the poem "Añoranza." In this version, the verses are typewritten as follows:

Por el aire bogaban palabras gruesas,
la voz de la guitarra saltaba entre las mozas,
chismeaban las maracas,
y el güiro despedía risotadas cargadas.

In the *Cuaderno* version, the "thick words" become "loose words," the guiro becomes an "old man arched with laughter" and the "maracas" disappear to make room for a longer verse. The spatial organization of verses also changes. In the earlier version of the poem "Humatas," the poetic voice pleads with greater strength that the barrio would allow him to remember it "just a little while longer." In the earlier version of "Carmen Dolores," the town is "small." Much of the conflict between the poetic voice and the town's "smallness" disappears over the approximately twenty years that separate these books. Many of the verses in *El Pueblo Oscuro* have been moved on the page, suggesting a willingness to play with graphic arrangement, which disappeared in *Cuaderno*.

Nostalgia includes a great deal of poems that Rivera Avilés would exclude completely from *Cuaderno*, but in this collection, rather than eliminate or edit poems he thought unworthy of publication, he simply crossed them out in their entirety, leaving "tracks" of his process scattered throughout the book. The result is a series of permissions, prohibitions, traces of a struggle, evidence of a pained relationship with and against the writing. Ten out of fourteen poems didn't make the cut.

---

11. "... porque estoy triste y viajo, /y conozco la tierra y estoy triste." Trans.
   "... because I am sad and I travel, / and I know the earth and am sad."

During this period, he also wrote a good deal of poetry and prose in English. Some of this writing was assigned as part of his university education. Other pieces seemed explorations of a language he had mostly learned to speak fluently, read, and write during his military service:

> I walk over maps during nights. Always alone, just with my understanding and my time, honestly living. Then I feel free of my skin, of my spaces, of the body I have to carry around daily.
>
> I live near the railroad tracks, so the trains that come and go during the high nights carry me everywhere. I never close the windows, for I enjoy discovering the emerging of the trains as they appear slowly growing in the silence, until they assassinate it with thunderous impetus, and then leave again dying peacefully along the perspective of my ears.

Here the "emerging" trains transport the poetic voice through the sound of their "thunderous impetus." The speaker also invites the movement of words into the body he has to "carry around daily." The trains' powerful "impetus" contrasts with the weight created, not just by the body, but also by the routine of the present, the dead weight of the "daily" life. These ideas reemerge throughout his work, as Rivera Avilés continues to set up contrasts between bodily immobility and a soul that wanders with ease, traveling through writing—by returning to a time before the war when the speaker could go "climbing pana trees"[12]—or through a poetics of nature—by harnessing with language the forces of rivers, hurricanes, and earthquakes. Whatever his relationship to English during this period, Rivera Avilés never stopped writing in Spanish, until he eventually abandoned the project of writing in any other language.

Later Works: *1963* and *Cuaderno de tierra y hombre* (1974)

Over the years, Rivera Avilés continued to write melancholic poems populated by the painful physical and psychological vestiges of war. One of the military records Castillo Beauchamp filed as part of the lawsuit, describes the symptoms Rivera Avilés suffered daily, which

---

12. See the poem "Humatas."

included "1. Acute post-traumatic stress syndrome; 2. Chronic post-traumatic stress syndrome; 3. Chronic neuropathy and chronic pain.; 4. Right foot drop; 5. Chronic stasis of his right leg and foot; 6. Pressure ulcer; 7. Chronic pain; 8. All consequent mental affection that necessarily occur following any amputation of any limb." When asked in an interview what would happen if Rivera Avilés did not "use alcohol at bedtime," Virginia stated that he "suffered nightmares and insomnia."

Descriptions of his varying corporal states would appear throughout the poems. Sometimes his body was an "old soldier's."[13] At other times, he experienced bodily pleasure or repose, as the speaker was able to "roam quietly under the tall trees."[14] There was a noticeable disjunction between the mobility of the poet's vision and his body's woundedness, which the poet associates time and time again with a present that does not belongs to either the Edenic nature of his past or the utopian paradise of the future. Most often, the speaker seems stuck in an eternal Groundhog Day, in a rural world populated by the imposed changes brought on by Puerto Rico's rapid modernization; the body manifests as a series of limitations all linked to war, which in turn the speaker associates with imperialism.

As attested to by the consistent appearance of these connections throughout his poetry, the war-related trauma and its effects seem to bear a traceable relation to the machinery of forced industrialization that tore asunder a mutually generative link between earth and self. In this sense, Rivera Avilés is part of a modernist tradition for which industrialization represents a break with nature and man's true being. Just as the machinery of war estranges the poet from his own body, so too the machinery of industry has alienated him from the body of his past, the body of his barrio, of its trees, and its "deep whispers."[15] The difference perhaps lies in the fact that, for Rivera Avilés, this relationship is not optional or passing, but rather foundational. His bodily estrangement is not metaphorical first, but rather corporeal first, becoming figurative when translated onto the page. Similarly, the rupture of earth and man is not something

---

13. See "Vestigios de pólvora/ Gunpowder Vestiges."

14. See "Epanáfora del vacío/ Anaphora of Emptiness."

15. See "Humatas."

he experiences as a witness, but rather as a displaced townsperson, forced to migrate due to poverty and colonialism, only to return to a world transformed for the worse.

We may find examples of this fragmentation brought on by tekné in his notebook/diary/ calendar/appointment book, which I have provisionally titled *1963*, since this is the year written on the cover. The journal begins with a series of quotidian descriptions listing parties, people, and errands. Progressively, some of the entries become more and more melancholic. The entry dated Monday, January 21 (no year), begins with the words "terrible day" and ends with the following description: "Everything is an amalgam of grim and lackluster afflictions. This bodes ill; I know something will happen that will not be to my benefit—God free me of this life that is so bitter, so rancid."[16] This entry is followed by two one-sentence descriptions of several events. These anti-entries are neither reminders nor narrations. What could have been gained by noting the day he began fixing the house or the day he visited a friend? Why are so many pages left blank? These are some of the many markers of Rivera Avilés' ongoing but irregular concern with memory and loss.

As the diary progresses, we also find various descriptions of the quantity of work or rest he had done during the day, but no specific descriptions of the work itself. Work could consist of errands, teaching, physical labor, writing, or any number of activities. Sparing in details, spreading his writing across the narrow page until the letters become indistinguishable, the exercise of writing seems to serve an arbitrary function. The irregularity of the entries suggest it was not a consistent source of relief or reminder, and the writing points to something beyond any functionality.

It is at this point in the journal that the poem entries begin. These no longer refer to acts that took place in the recent past, but seem like first drafts jotted down on here because of the notebook's physical accessibility rather than according to any organizational principle. Yet that does not explain why none of these fragments ever made it into his books. It is as if they belong here, in this notebook and nowhere else. The days left blank, the refusal to use

16. "Todo una amalgama de aflicciones torvas y deslucidas. Esto va mal; sé que algo va a ocurrir que no será para mi bien—Dios me libre de esta vida tan agria, tan rancia."

accurate dates, the insistence on correcting the book's ordained structure seem to offer us a poetics attentive to loss and tender in its fragmentation. Rivera Avilés does not distinguish between daily dealings and his poems. They are both bound by commonness and its "dirty clarities."[17]

In *Cuaderno de tierra y hombre*, which won the Premio Ventana, earth/land ("tierra") and man ("hombre") are made w(hole)[18] again. The poems were written from 1956-1973, and the book includes poems that date back to his early works. They are joined in the dedication by the themes that reappear throughout his work: "*To Humatas—passion of the past;/ To my wife and children—passion of the present;/ To the future—passion of Poetry;/ To the Earth— timeless passion.*" Humatas, the barrio of his childhood, and poetry stood outside the realm of the present, each one step away from the elemental wholeness for which he strove and which permeated his work: the earth/land.

In fact, his poem "Humatas" from *Cuaderno* inverts the journey from the country to the city by bringing the lost youth of his barrio into the present, like a recovered memory. Invoking a shared life, the speaker asks a personified Humatas to allow him to romanticize their now estranged relationship:

> ...Y tu mirada verde para todos los días
> (cuando se abrían tus manos de pájaros y flores
> y las cabras mordían los gritos del rocío).
>
> Entonces tú tendrías doce años, Humatas,
> y mis pies rastreaban tus veredas y ríos
> y tus jaldas mis uñas llenaban de colores.
>
> ...And your gaze, green for all time,
> (when your bird and flower hands would open
> and goats would bite the dew's screams).

---

17. See "Elegía major a la tierra/ Major Elegy to the Earth."
18. See Fred Moten. *In the Break: The Aesthetics of Black Radical Tradition*. Minneapolis: U of Minnesota, 2003.

Then you'd be about twelve, Humatas,
and my feet would track your paths and rivers
and your mountains' laps would paint my nails.

In the last stanza, it becomes clear that the speaker is in the city. The place and date at the bottom of the poem indicate that it was written while Rivera Avilés was attending San Mateo College in 1956. It is not clear if the speaker is referring to San Mateo itself as the "city," since San Mateo in 1956 was hardly a city (unless we view it as a city in relation to the size of Añasco) and Rivera Avilés had surely seen more than one city since joining the Navy. Here various temporalities and locations are folded into the poem. There is the past in which the speaker and Humatas share a youth and there is the present of memory in which the speaker is expressing nostalgia, which in itself could be one of two presents: the present in when the poem is published (now past) and during which the speaker (assuming there is an overlap with the poet) is living in the city of San Mateo, or a present that is being remembered in San Mateo in the year 1956, in which the speaker inhabiting a series of cities that have blended into the prepositional phrase "de ciudad." Then there is the possibility that speaker and poet diverge in the poem, despite their initial overlap, and that the present is even more general, a period of time that initiates with his hospitalization and is cut off from a prewar past. This folding or delayed time near the end of the poem is marked by a figurative reenactment of a traumatic rupture.

Much like William Wordsworth's "Ode: Intimations of Immortality from Recollections of Early Childhood," the loss of childhood is accompanied by the trauma of awakening. During his studies at San Mateo College, Rivera Avilés became familiar with Wordsworth,[19] yet his relationship to the English Romantic poet's work is disidentificatory.[20] There are no "jatacas" or "hamacas" in

---

19. I have reached this conclusion after examining the books held in his private collection and finding several anthologies with poetry by Wordsworth that he had acquired during his California years.

20. See José Esteban Muñoz. *Disidentifications: Queers of Color and the Performance of Politics.* Minneapolis: U of Minnesota, 1999.

Wordsworth's bucolic scene just as there are no "cataracts [that] blow their trumpets" in Añasco. Both treat the earth as somewhat maternal, but, while Wordsworth names her explicitly saying she has "a Mother's mind," Rivera Avilés never names it as such, and in fact "barrio" is masculine, making Humatas' gender fluctuant. The inverted voyage of memory eventually circles back to the city where the speaker is situated. Many of his poems end with the speaker experiencing disillusionment and loss through a similar kind of re-embodiment. He returns from his voyage of memory to a wounded body that has been estranged from the wholeness of the pre-sexed "earth." Not only does he feel nostalgia for a lost childhood, but also for the "ambiguity" of childhood that precedes a war that bound him to a gendered role. But more importantly, the poem reenacts the mistake of not having foreseen how his enlistment in the Marines would cause him to irrevocably lose his childhood in Humatas.

Up to this point, I've been addressing the speaker as a universal, but, in many senses, this is what Rivera Avilés worked against. Within a discourse in which impoverished subjects were held up as examples of the failures of a responsible Puerto Rican intellectual class, he often positioned himself as both speaker and poet. He went further than pointing at the impossibility of total recuperation and also signaled that his own access to discourse was mediated by and necessitated loss. As a Black, disabled veteran within an ableist, masculinist, racist discourse, his writing reproduced difference-in-repetition. By pointing at the erasure of his childhood self, he further indicated that the child's death became the prerequisite for his adult participation in an exclusionary discourse.[21]

Rivera Avilés' poetry, reenacts loss as a means of remembering more than a dead childhood and brings to life a rootedness in a working-class politics that precedes his access to literature. His memory of Humatas is bound to his active anti-imperialism, his hatred of U.S. government funded wars, his refusal to identify with a complicit ruling class, and his resistance to the ableist world that greeted him upon his return. The

---

21. See my doctoral dissertation: Salas Rivera, Raquel, "The Fetish of the Self-Translator: Self-Translation in the Work of Sotero Rivera Avilés and Ángela María Dávila" (2019). *Publicly Accessible Penn Dissertations*. 3401.

poet enacted an awakening that extended beyond nostalgia for a rural childhood into a critique of power.[22]

Despite his interest in rooting himself in the past, his poetry does not feel constrained. It fascinated me from a young age, in part because his writing seemed simultaneously elusive and concrete, as if the reader were as much an accomplice as a stranger amongst the speaker's narajanos, jatacas, and townspeople, leaving me with the sense that I had not read a particular poem well enough, despite its seeming simplicity. The speaker is at times a pícaro, an old man living out his days in the town of his youth, a young boy crossing fields, a soldier in Korea, a poet speaking to another poet, or an aspiring revolutionary. The poems range in tone, yet a voice carries through in his consistent use of figurative language based on quotidian rural experiences.

---

22. Robert McRuer's *Crip Theory* has shaped disability studies and influenced my understanding of Rivera Avilés' life and poetry, but using it as a framework for Rivera Avilés' work has been difficult. I found Leah Lakshmi Piepzna-Samarasinha's 2018 *Care Work* far more useful and am thankful for this pivotal book. To decolonize crip, queer, feminist theory, we have to move beyond the transhistorical universalizing frameworks of colonialism and foreground crip voices from colonial contexts. In Rivera Avilés' case, it is impossible to understand his relationship to an able-bodied past without understanding the colonial relationship between Puerto Rico and the United States and the development of post-war masculinity. Still, his conditional inclusion in the canon was to a certain extent permissible, precisely because of his willingness to translate his pre-war, pre-literary experiences into a standardized dialect of Spanish. His use of words such as "dethroned" ("destronada") and "disturbing" ("alborotando"), belonged to the literary discourse of his time, not to the young boy from Humatas who was about to enlist in the Navy. The irony that permeates Rivera Avilés' work springs from an acute bitterness with the cost of access to middle-class intellectual spheres. He saw his disabilities as directly linked to this access. He had come to depend on his writing as a prothesis that could help him gain access to a pre-wounded self, thereby developing a contradictory and complex relationship to literature, one in which the literary was both a prized portal to other possible worlds (including his past) and a shut-off discourse only available to a few who had capital, or who, like himself, paid a high entrance fee.

Through a singularity of style and a refusal to write for anyone or anything other than his own guiding aesthetic principles, Sotero Rivera Avilés was a poet, through and through. His only church was poetry. As is evident with poems such as his homage to Che Guevara, he had clearly aligned political beliefs, but via poetry he ultimately questioned all forms of authority. He would edify a statue in one poem and ironize all forms of idealization in the next, producing a rich, multilayered collection by one of the most unique and unparalleled poets I have read. It is my hope that this edition will inspire future readers and scholars to further critically engage with his writing.

On Selecting and Translating Sotero Rivera Avilés

A month after my father passed away and two weeks after I started taking testosterone, and thanks to a translation fellowship from the National Endowment for the Arts, the first work I fully resumed were these translations. It felt obvious and prosaic to start here, with the figure whose tangles had defined our family, through defiance, disidentification, or partial acceptance. My hope, since I undertook this work, has been to lean into my obsession with my grandfather's life, and accept my desire to see myself, my queerness, and my transness in his successful and failed attempts at upholding societal expectations.

Earlier, I described my grandfather's return to Puerto Rico as a "return to a world transformed for the worse." In some ways, my return to Puerto Rico after almost eight years in Philadelphia has felt similar. As I write this, the cost of rent in the San Juan area has significantly increased thanks to a new wave of settler colonialism that has brought many U.S. Americans here in search of gold, beaches, and paradise. Although my life and my grandfather's life were different enough to feel foreign, in translating his poetry, I have experienced a shared sadness at coming back to a world that seems forever altered by outside forces. Unlike abuelito, I do not think of my childhood or my past, including him, with nostalgia. This project has been as much about demystifying my grandfather, through research and study, as it has been about honoring him.

I say I "resumed" this work because I had really begun these translations slightly before moving to pursue my Ph.D. in Comparative Literature and Literary Theory at the University of Pennsylvania. In fact, many early versions became part of my doctoral dissertation and led me to conduct my first family interviews and look through some of the archival materials I used for this book. It was the guidance and encouragement of my dissertation committee—Emily Wilson, Kevin Platt, and especially Julio Ramos—that convinced me I had to pursue these translations and the accompanying research. The committee was kind and critical without being harsh, and saw the shimmer in my early work. I mention this tenderness because it taught me the kind of care I should take with a history of my grandfather's life, not just because of familial expectations or obligations, but rather because the care we take with others, our living and our dead, makes the building blocks for a better world.

These translations are also an inventory of many Soteros. Here is Sotero, the Puerto Rican poet who died of hunger in a bakery. Here, the hemorrhaging boxer with his skull cracked open by war; Sotero, with his Puerto Rican syndrome;[23] Sotero, the fisherman swallowed by the sea before returning to Mazatlán; Sotero, Añasco's last hanged man; Sotero, who cried over onions, dead in cold Madrid; Sotero, the satisfied patriarch of old age. This selection includes his poems and my translations; his real lives and his missed deaths. These cling with the insolvency of memorials. I have tried to the best of my ability to become proximate through interviews, research, and patchwork. One of these dead men is real, a family legend. One of these was a great orator against finality, a self-mythologizer, a poet.

Given how little time we spent together (I was eight when he passed away), I can only describe my memories of Sotero Rivera Avilés as hauntings. It is through my uncles, my mother, my aunt, and especially my grandmother, Virginia, that I have patched together different versions of who he was. My grandmother describes a yellow house by a river in Humatas. My mother swears he slept

---

23. See Gherovici, Patricia. *The Puerto Rican Syndrome*. New York, NY: Other, 2003. I often think about the fact that there was no PTSD diagnosis for veterans like my grandfather and that this racist syndrome existed specifically to pathologize Puerto Rican veterans. As Gherovici notes, the diagnosis shares characteristics with past descriptions of hysteria, lending credence to my theory that a doubling down on performative masculinity may well have been a response to a violent diagnosis and the threat of becoming an experimental subject.

on the floor. They argue, agree, then sit in the living room confused, neither one admitting they may have forgotten. This happens on one of many trips I took to Mayagüez during these past two years in order to interview my family about my grandfather and fact check some of the stories I had heard them tell over the years. Like his memories of Humatas, my family's memories of Sotero are plagued by nostalgia, distance, desire, and inevitable decay.

Rather than lament all loss, I have taken this as a jumping off point for a book-length reflection on the potentialities and limits of recovery projects. Some things need to be left behind and forgotten. We can't spend our lives living under the shadows of our elders. Other things must be remembered if we are to reimagine the futures we inherit. As I understand it, the best translations do both, they release and cling in the right places. These traces that resist oblivion, must be, in the words of the poet Jack Spicer, "led across time, not preserved against it."[24] And, like Spicer, I speak with dead men, or at least one dead man, in order to understand how I came to poetry, why I guard the idea that something incommensurable happens in the poem. For my grandfather, poetry was when his life began, but in order to become a poet, a past self had to die in that hospital in California. A self that nonetheless haunted almost all of his poems. This is essentially a kind of transition, a kind of translation.

These poems themselves feel haunted: by the war, by his childhood, by friendships, travels, and girlfriends. In translating "Domingo sin iglesia/ Churchless Sunday," I retrace his steps, from his artificial arm on the couch, to his backyard, to the window facing the street, and finally to the church. I retrace his movements, his gestures. He "can laugh like an aimless shoe,/ destroyed,/ thrown to nights and rain" at the "the priest and old women/ that raise their rage and destroy pulpits/ if they see too few sinners." But my favorite gesture is his shift from commonplace artifice, which he often describes as a sort of welcome failure, to a divinity he saw as hypocritical. His artificial arm laughs because it "understands" modernity's obsession with usefulness and goodness is doomed to ruin. It is this exhausted refusal—that of a veteran's artificial arm—that stays with me in my recent grief.

---

24. See Jack Spicer, and Peter Gizzi. *After Lorca*. New York Review Books, 2021.

It is also this arm that I played with as a child, that he handed to me, that led me to pull at my own arm in an effort to take it off. It planted the idea in my mind that bodies were not all the same, that some parts could be made different, even removed, something profoundly radical for a young trans person to come to understand.

If the poems are hauntings, then the translations are hauntings of hauntings. The Spanish filmmaker José Val del Omar, for *Variaciones sobre una granada*, would take innumerable photos of a pomegranate (in Spanish "granada," like the city of his birth) with different lenses and filters. Sometimes he'd film and then take a photo. The effect was accumulative: a phenomenological pile-up. This was his way of looking for the unity he called God, the essence of the pomegranate. Perhaps, through my translations, I am driven by a similar impossibility: the desire to sense in other languages, through other filters, my grandfather's poems, and layer them on top of each other until he feels present.

Some translated verses have left me unsatisfied. In the poem "Domingo sin iglesia/ Churchless Sunday," the verse "pasan bajo el calor de mi ventana" became "pass beneath my window's warmth." I imagine the nuns suffering under their frocks in the Caribbean heat, but "calor" remits to human warmth, even tenderness, those things—like the smell of used books and towels and the entangled scent of incense—that are of the flesh. "El calor de mi cuerpo" would translate as "my body's heat," and "el calor de mi ventana" makes the window itself a body between two bodies (a translator) or the trace of a body between two worlds (a ghost). Still, I feel the translation begins in a way he would have loved. To the carelessness of "echado sin reparos," I add the indeterminate adjective "some." He did say "un mueble" not "algún mueble," but in a small house can you really say "a couch" and not "the couch" without implying indeterminacy? It would be as strange as saying "a child" to the child who lives with you every day, sitting on the shared couch, playing on the brown tiled floor you sweep almost daily.

Then there are stylistic details I haven't quite found a way to bring into English: "en el patio de entonces," has a musicality I aimed for with "in what was once my yard." "De entonces" is comparative. It implies a "back-then" versus "now" yard. Yet, "my back-then yard" sounds like something you could get at a hardware store and lacks the nostalgic drift of the Spanish wording. Here, there is no satisfying path, the tracks stop dead and I have to retrace my journey and find "another way/ for our dark town," which we have built together in these poems and translations. The title of "Historia para otra historia" becomes "Story for Another History" in English, and though I am unable to find a way to mirror the subtle shift from lowercase to capital letter that makes the difference between "History" and "story," I think that "his" here is suggestive in another way, for it is our history he has written, ours and his.

The book you hold in your hands contains two poetry books and my translations in their entirety: *El Pueblo Obscuro y una puerta al jardín* and *Cuaderno de tierra y hombre*. It also contains poetic fragments from his notebook *1963* and selected poems from *Nada pierdes, caballo viejo (Faena de remedios)*. I did not include his first two collections, *Nostalgia* and *Abandonos*. Although significantly powerful, many of those early poems seemed to find their final form in *El pueblo oscuro* and *Cuaderno*. As for his final collection, *Nada pierdes, caballo viejo (Faena de remedios)*, it feels like a collection of poems and not necessarily a poetry book. In this it is similar to *Nostalgia* and *Abandonos*, but it differs from these in that the poems are clearly the work of a poet with a mature voice and style. For this reason, I chose to select some of my favorite poems from this final collection and placed it before *Cuaderno*, his most well-developed book.

After much consideration, I chose not to offer definitions for words such as "pajuil," "jataca," or "hicaco." Some are the names of fruits and cultural practices that are autochthonous (though not always exclusive) to Puerto Rico. I did not translate these terms because to do so would be to establish false equivalencies, much like the Spanish conquistadores who named flora and fauna they came across after familiar European plants and animals. I made exceptions in those cases where it would be difficult for most researchers to find the necessary information to make sense of my use in English. This is the case, for example, of "choferes públicos," a practice that requires some contextualization, even in Spanish.

I'd like to thank the National Endowment for the Arts for granting me the translation fellowship that made this work possible. I am grateful to the Action Books Blog for publishing early versions of "Brief Elegy to a Fallen Brother," "Gunpowder Vestiges," "Anaphora of Emptiness," "Churchless Sunday," and "Monday, July 22." I'm also grateful to *Poetry Daily* for publishing a section of this essay. I'd like to thank my friends for their support while I became a hermit, always promising to see them "soon, soon." Special thanks to Ricardo Ferrer Antunez for his insights, for the laughter, and for the late nights. Thank you, Circumference Books, and, in particular, Jennifer Kronovet for believing in this project. Without my cousin, Miguel Alvelo Rivera, who shares a passion for my grandfather and his work, I would not have a collection of new images of Humatas, taken in our most recent family visit as we searched for our grandfather's ashes. Thank you Neftali, Yamil, Emir, Sandra, and Sofía for allowing me to undertake this delicate and tender piece of our family's history. I, of course, have to thank Yolanda Rivera Castillo, madre querida, who has always guided me and who passed down a love of poetry from grandfather, to mother, to me. Finally, we have come to the biggest thank you of all. Gracias, gracias, gracias, abuelita, Virginia Castillo Beauchamp, espero que te guste este poemario de abuelito y mi selección, traté de hacerle justicia y sin ti esto no hubiese sido posible.

Raquel Salas Rivera
Santurce, Puerto Rico
May 12, 2022

Biographies

Sotero Rivera Avilés

Sotero Rivera Avilés was a poet, critic, novelist, and essayist born in 1933 in Añasco, Puerto Rico. He co-founded the group Mester de poetas and the literary journal *homónima* (1967). His early works include various poetry books: *Nostalgia* (1957), *Abandonos* (1958), the unpublished typewritten manuscript *El Pueblo Obscuro y una puerta al jardín* (unknown date), and a journal titled *1963*. In 1974 Rivera Avilés won the Premio Ventana for *Cuaderno de tierra y hombre*. Two years later he published the critical study, *La generación del 60: Aproximaciones a tres autores* (Instituto de Cultura Puertorriqueña, 1976). It was followed by the publication of *Nada pierdes, caballo viejo (Faena de remedios)* in 1989. He passed away in 1994, leaving behind a wife, five children, and three grandchildren who became astronomers, poets, linguists, nature conservationists, psychologists, actors, singers, engineers, historians, and educators. His body was cremated and his ashes were scattered over the mountains overlooking Humatas.